THE
MUSEUMS
—— OF ——
ISRAEL

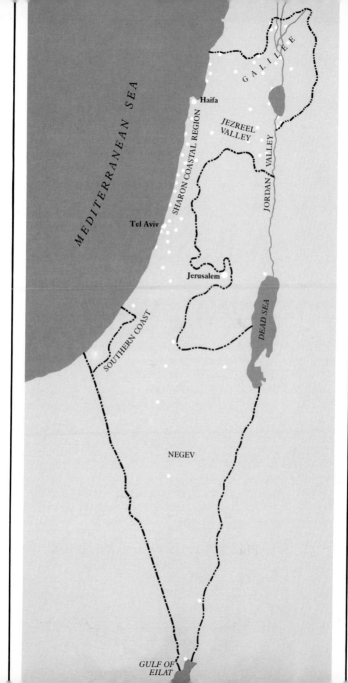

THE
MUSEUMS
—— OF ——
ISRAEL

By Nitza Rosovsky
and Joy Ungerleider-Mayerson

Photographs by David Harris

Harry N. Abrams, Inc., Publishers, New York

For Henry and Philip

Editor: Ruth Eisenstein
Designers: Dirk Luykx, Lydia Gershey, Yonah Schurink
Maps by Wilhelmina Reyinga-Amrhein

Photographs by David Harris except for the following: page 19,
Garo Nalbandian, Courtesy Studium Biblicum Franciscanum
Museum; page 31, Vivienne Silver; page 63, left, Yoram Lehman;
page 66, bottom, Courtesy Tel Dan Excavations; page 71, Courtesy
Professor Nahman Avigad; pages 90–93, Courtesy Eretz Israel
Museum; page 104, Courtesy Tel Aviv Museum of Art; page 105,
A. Hai, Courtesy Tel Aviv Museum of Art; pages 106–8, Courtesy
Tel Aviv Museum of Art; pages 158–59, Courtesy Hecht Museum;
page 164, Courtesy Museum of Japanese Art; page 239, Courtesy
Museum for Beduin Culture.

Library of Congress Cataloging-in-Publication Data

Rosovsky, Nitza.
The museums of Israel.

1. Museums—Israel—Directories. I. Ungerleider-
Mayerson, Joy. II. Title.
AM79.I8R67   1989   069'.025'5694   88–7399
ISBN 0-8109-2422-6

A Times Mirror Company

Printed and bound in Hong Kong

CONTENTS

THE MUSEUMS

PREFACE

Some 120 museums are scattered throughout Israel, a country equal in size to the state of New Jersey. There is a passion for museums in Israel, a passion for preserving and interpreting the past, understandable in this old-new land. The countryside—a museum without walls—is filled with remains. Many kibbutzim and agricultural settlements have created museums for the antiquities uncovered in their fields, others for specimens of local flora and fauna. Fifty of the country's museums exhibit archaeology, forty history, either exclusively or in company with other categories. Some museums are devoted to a single topic—the history of an era, the folklore of a region, the work of a local artist. For the purposes of this book, the authors have adhered to the definition of a museum as stated by the International Council of Museums (ICOM): A permanent institution which collects, conserves, and displays, for study, education, and enjoyment, collections of objects of cultural or scientific significance.

The organizing principle behind this guidebook is to provide information about these cultural resources, large and small—many of which are not frequented even by Israelis and are unknown to visitors. In addition to the practical details—location, hours, telephone number, admission fee—the special strengths of each museum are indicated. The book is divided into eight regions, with maps for each area and for the large cities. It directs visitors not only to the larger and more famous museums but also to the smaller, lesser-known, and more intimate museums, which offer a totally different experience. It should be mentioned here that many of the antiquities exhibited in the museums of Israel, including those described and illustrated in this book, are the property of the Israel Department of Antiquities and Museums.

The authors have visited each one of the 120 museums described. The book is more than a guide because it encompasses the history of the country, recent archaeological discoveries, the ethnography of the diverse population, and the vitality of the current art scene. With the help of the photographs, mostly by David Harris, even an armchair reader can enjoy the museums without ever leaving home. As for travelers, this book reminds them that wherever they are in Israel there is a museum nearby, usually worth a detour!

It will be noted that in some cases visitors are advised to telephone ahead. Owing to budgetary constraints, some of the small museums are not open at regular hours; a call in advance will unlock doors and may even lead to a guided tour by the founder of, or moving spirit behind, the museum. At the helm of a number of Israeli museums are nonprofessionals whose knowledge and dedication more than compensate for the absence of formal training and titles.

Certain inconsistencies in the spelling of museum names are the result of following the museums' own preferences with regard to transliteration. In listing the visiting hours of the museums, a simplified form of the twenty-four-hour system has been used. Since hours (and admission fees) are subject to change, it is wise to call ahead to avoid disappointment.

As aids to the reader/traveler, three lists are appended to the text: Museums by Subject (page 249), Museums Listed Alphabetically (page 253), and Museum Locations (page 255). The new Israeli museums that are in the planning stages as this book goes to press will be welcomed into future editions.

ACKNOWLEDGMENTS

It is indeed a pleasure for us to express our sincere thanks to our colleagues in the museum world who have given so generously of their time and counsel. We have been personally rewarded by our association with those many individuals whose dedication and extraordinary effort brought some of the small museums of Israel into being. We should also like to give special thanks to David Amiran, Magen Broshi, Ruth Hestrin, Irene Lewitt, Rutha Peled, and Avner Shalev for their timely assistance. We are ever grateful to Trude and Moshe Dothan, who helped unlock closed doors in remote corners of the country. We extend our appreciation to Neil A. Silberman for his contribution. Working with David Harris has been heartwarming, not only because of the superb quality of his photographs but also because of his continuous involvement in and enthusiasm for the project. And to Ruth Eisenstein, our wise and tireless editor at Harry N. Abrams, Inc., our deepest gratitude for her remarkable skills, expertise, and insights.

N.R.
J.U.-M.

CHRONOLOGY

The chronology of ancient Israel is subject to continual revision in view of new archaeological discoveries. The dates given here for the early periods are those most commonly used in Israel.

STONE AGE	1,500,000 Years Before Present–4500 BC

| PALEOLITHIC | 1,500,000 Years Before Present–10,300 BC |
| NATUFIAN CULTURE | c. 10,300–8500 BC |

Advance from hunting and food-gathering to agriculture

| NEOLITHIC | c. 8500–4500 BC |

Systematic cultivation of land; making of pottery

CHALCOLITHIC	c. 4500–3150 BC

Advanced crafts appear; beginning of metal industry

BRONZE AGE (CANAANITE)	3150–1200 BC

| EARLY BRONZE / CANAANITE | 3150–2200 BC |

First cities are built; trade links with Egypt and Mesopotamia

| MIDDLE BRONZE / CANAANITE | 2200–1550 BC |

Beginning of the alphabet; developed urban cultures

| LATE BRONZE / CANAANITE | 1550–1200 BC |

Exodus of Israelites from Egypt and settlement in Canaan

IRON AGE (ISRAELITE)	1200–586 BC

Period of the Judges
Sea Peoples settle in coastal plain

Saul anointed first king of Israel	c. 1020 BC
David rules Israel	c. 1000–960 BC
Solomon reigns over Israel and builds Temple in Jerusalem	c. 960–922 BC

First Temple Period	c. 960–586 BC

Beginning of Divided Monarchy: Judah in the south, Israel in the north	c. 922 BC
Prophets: Hosea, Amos, Micah	8th century BC
Prophet: Isaiah	c. 700 BC

Assyrian kings Shalmaneser V and Sargon II attack and conquer

northern kingdom of Israel	724–721 BC
Assyrian king Sennacherib campaigns against King Hezekiah of Judah	701 BC
Prophet Jeremiah	c. 625–586 BC
Nebuchadnezzar destroys Jerusalem and Temple; ends Kingdom of Judah; exiles Jews to Babylon	586 BC

PERSIAN PERIOD — 586–332 BC

| One year after conquering the Babylonians, Cyrus allows Jews to return from exile | 538 BC |
| Second Temple is rebuilt under Zerubbabel | 520 BC |

Second Temple Period — 520 BC–AD 70

| Ezra goes to Jerusalem | 458 BC |
| Nehemiah follows Ezra, rebuilds city's walls | 445 BC |

HELLENISTIC PERIOD — 332–63 BC

| Alexander the Great conquers the country | 332 BC |
| Antiochus IV of Syria desecrates the Temple and outlaws practice of Judaism | 167 BC |

Hasmonean (Maccabee) Period — 167–37 BC

| Hasmonean (Maccabee) revolt | 167 BC |
| Judah Maccabee captures Jerusalem; rededicates Temple | 164 BC |

ROMAN PERIOD — 63 BC–AD 324

| Roman general Pompey subjugates Judea | 63 BC |

Herodian Period — 37 BC–AD 70

Herod conquers Jerusalem; Rome proclaims him King of Judea	37 BC
Herod enlarges and beautifies the Temple; builds palaces and cities, including Caesarea and its port	37–4 BC
Life of Jesus	c. 7 BC–AD 29
Pontius Pilate procurator of Judea	AD 26–36
First Revolt of the Jews against Rome	67–73
Vespasian conquers Galilee	67
Titus, son of Vespasian, destroys the Temple and city of Jerusalem	70
Masada falls to the Romans	73

Yavneh serves as center of Jewish learning | 70–132
Second Jewish Revolt against Rome, led by Bar Kokhba | 132–35
Emperor Hadrian rebuilds Jerusalem, renaming city Aelia Capitolina, country Palestine | 135
Majority of Jewish population moves north to Galilee | 136–600
Codifying of the Mishna (oral law) completed | c. 200

Age of the Mishna and Talmud · c. 200–500

Tiberias becomes Jewish spiritual center | c. 235

BYZANTINE PERIOD · 324–640

Emperor Constantine legalizes Christianity | 313
Constantine becomes sole ruler of empire | 324
Helena, Constantine's mother, visits Holy Land to identify and enshrine Christian sites; emperor erects Church of Holy Sepulchre | 326–35
Palestinian Talmud completed in Galilee | c. 500
Persians conquer Palestine | 614
Byzantine Emperor Heraclius recaptures Palestine | 628

EARLY ARAB / MUSLIM PERIOD · 640–1099

Conquest of Palestine by Muslims; Caliph Omar visits Jerusalem | 638
Abd el-Malek builds Dome of the Rock on Temple Mount | 691
El-Aqsa Mosque is completed by el-Walid el-Malek | 715
Power shift from Umayyads of Damascus to Abbasids of Baghdad; the Abbasids continue to enhance Jerusalem | 750
Seljuk invasion | 1071

CRUSADER PERIOD · 1099–1291

Conquest of Palestine by Crusaders | 1099
Crusaders build castles, abbeys, and churches. Major repairs to Church of Holy Sepulchre completed | 1149
Saladin (Salah ed-Din) defeats Crusaders at the Horns of Hattin | 1187
Mongols sack Palestine | 1244
Mamluks capture Acre, last Crusader stronghold | 1291

MAMLUK PERIOD · 1291–1517

Byzantium/Constantinople conquered by Ottomans | 1453
Jews begin to arrive in country after Spanish exile | 1492

OTTOMAN/TURKISH PERIOD   1517–1918

Conquest of Palestine	1516–17
Sultan Suleiman the Magnificent restores the walls of Jerusalem	1538
Invasion of Palestine by Napoleon	1799
Mohammed Ali of Egypt rules country, allows foreign powers to open consulates in Jerusalem	1831–40
Petah Tikva, first modern agricultural settlement, is founded by Jews from Jerusalem	1878
The Biluim (first Zionist immigrants) arrive in Palestine	1882
Theodor Herzl meets Kaiser Wilhelm II in Jerusalem	1898
Tel Aviv founded	1909
Many Jews exiled from Palestine by Turks during World War I	1914–17

BRITISH MANDATE PERIOD   1920–1948

Balfour Declaration	Nov. 2, 1917
Jerusalem surrenders to General Allenby	1917
British Army conquers Palestine	1918
The Mandate for Palestine is conferred on Great Britain by League of Nations	1920
Arab-Jewish disturbances	1921 and 1929
	1936–39
Clandestine immigration begins, by sea and land	1934
Lord Peel's Commission proposes partition of Palestine and limiting Jewish immigration	1937
British White Paper further curtails Jewish immigration and prohibits sale of land to Jews	May 17, 1939
United Nations resolution for partition of Palestine adopted	Nov. 29, 1947

STATE OF ISRAEL   1948

Israel's proclamation of Independence	May 14, 1948
Official termination of British Mandate; Arab states invade Israel	May 15, 1948
Israel War of Independence	1948–49
Chaim Weizmann first president of Israel	1948–52
Sinai Campaign	Oct. 1956
Six Day War	June 1967
Yom Kippur War	Oct. 1973
Israel–Egypt Peace Treaty	March 26, 1979

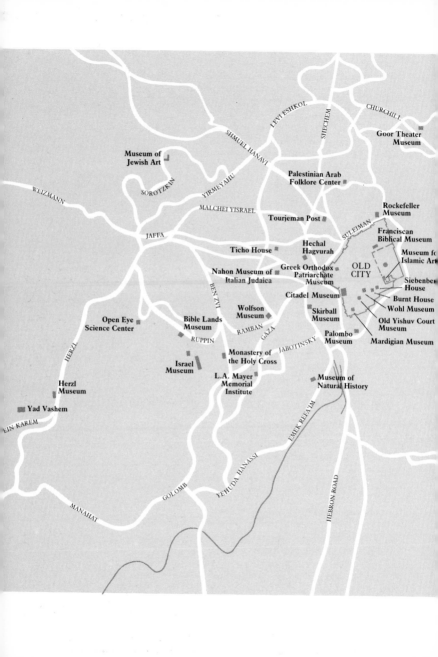

Goor Theater
Museum

CHURCHILL

LEVI ESHKOL

SHECHEM

SHMUEL HANAVI

Museum of
Jewish Art

SOROTZKIN

YIRMEYAHU

Palestinian Arab
Folklore Center

WEIZMANN

MALCHEI YISRAEL

Rockefeller
Museum

Tourjeman Post

JAFFA

SULEIMAN

Franciscan
Biblical Museum

Ticho House

Hechal
Hagvurah

Museum for
Islamic Art

Nahon Museum of
Italian Judaica

Greek Orthodox
Patriarchate
Museum

OLD
CITY

BEN ZVI

Siebenberg
House

Citadel Museum

Burnt House

Wolfson
Museum

Skirball
Museum

Wohl Museum

Open Eye
Science Center

Bible Lands
Museum

RAMBAN

GAZA

Old Yishuv Court
Museum

HERZL

RUPPIN

JABOTINSKY

Palombo
Museum

Mardigian Museum

Israel
Museum

Monastery of
the Holy Cross

Herzl
Memorial
Museum

L.A. Mayer
Memorial
Institute

Museum of
Natural History

Yad Vashem

EIN KAREM

EMEK REFA IM

GOLOMB

YEHUDA HANASSI

HEBRON ROAD

MANAHAT

JERUSALEM

THE BURNT HOUSE/HOUSE OF KATHROS

13 Tiferet Yisrael Street
Jewish Quarter, Old City
Jerusalem

HOURS: Sun.–Thurs. 9–17, Fri. 9–13

TEL.: 02–287211
ADMISSION: $2.00
(includes admission to the Wohl Museum)

Focus: **Jerusalem, AD 70**

The Burnt House, located in the heart of the Jewish Quarter in the Old City, combines the drama of a historical event with the excitement of an archae-

Storage jars and cooking vessels, end of Second Temple period

ological dig. Seen here are the excavated rooms of a house that belonged to an aristocratic Jewish family at the end of the Second Temple period, as well as a small collection of artifacts uncovered during the archaeological work. Together, this historic site and mini-museum convey a sense of the human tragedy that occurred here in AD 70: the destruction of Jerusalem by the Romans, one of the most disastrous events in Jewish history.

The Burnt House was discovered in 1970 by an archaeological team directed by Professor Nahman Avigad on behalf of the Israel Exploration Society, the Department of Antiquities and Museums of the Israel Ministry of Education and Culture, and the Hebrew University of Jerusalem. The finds uncovered here confirm the accounts of the Jewish historian Josephus, who was an eyewitness to the Roman siege and conquest of Jerusalem. The Upper City, where this house was located, remained in Jewish hands even after the destruction of the Temple, which took place on the 9th day of the month of Av. It was only a month later, on the 8th of Elul, that the Romans completed their destruction of the city, and the finds exhibited at the Burnt House give evidence of the violence and brutality with which it was carried out.

From the entrance, at street level, a stairway descends to the enclosed and preserved basement rooms of the ancient structure, which apparently served as storerooms or workshops. A large photomural shows the area as it was before the excavations began. To the left of the main display area is a large drainage tunnel, built on the bedrock, of the type that Josephus described as providing secret escape routes for the inhabitants of the besieged city. One room was not restored; its floor is covered with broken pottery, ashes, and charred beams just as it was on the day when the house burned down.

An iron spear, now on display, was found in the debris of the collapsed house, as was the skeletal arm of a young woman (which has since been buried, in accordance with Jewish law). A stone weight (one of a graduated series) bearing the inscription "Bar Kathros" in Aramaic, also found in the ruins, enabled the archaeologists to identify the owners of the house as a prominent family of priests mentioned in the Babylonian Talmud. Other artifacts in the display cases shed light on daily life in Jerusalem in the 1st century AD. They include painted pottery vessels, glass and pottery perfume bottles, a ceramic inkwell, basalt mortars and pestles, stone weights, and even a mold for casting coins. Within the excavation area itself, several stone tables and a number of large storage jars that have been pieced together are set up at the place of their discovery.

An excellent 15-minute slide show (with English presentations four times daily) covers events in Jerusalem at the end of the Second Temple period and gives a detailed account of the archaeological work carried out here.

THE CITADEL MUSEUM
OF THE HISTORY OF JERUSALEM

Tower of David, Old City
Jerusalem

HOURS: Sun.–Thurs. 8:30–16:30, Fri. 8:30–14   TEL.: 02–286079 or 02–286511

ADMISSION: $2.50

Focus: **Archaeology and History of Jerusalem; Architecture of the Citadel**

The Citadel is both a municipal museum and one of the city's most interesting historical sites. As Jerusalem's main fortress and military garrison for more than 2,000 years, the Citadel gives evidence of the presence of all the city's conquerors. Its eclectic architecture and the artifacts exhibited in some of its interior halls reflect the long and turbulent history of Jerusalem from the 2nd century BC to the present.

The Citadel is popularly known as the Tower of David, although it has no connection with the biblical king, whose city was located to the south of the Old City walls. The name originated in the mistaken belief of Christian pilgrims, beginning in the 4th century AD, that only David could have built so large and impressive a structure. In the 7th century AD, when the Muslims conquered Jerusalem, the Byzantine tradition was continued with their identification of the site as Mihrab Daud (Prayer Place of David). By the Crusader period, in the 12th century AD, the name had taken its modern form: on Crusader coins and maps it appears as Turris David (Lat. Tower of David).

Archaeological excavations around the Citadel and within the courtyard have revealed the complex history of this fortress. The oldest visible remains are walls and a defense tower built by the Maccabean kings of Judea in the 2nd century BC. A more imposing architectural feature is the base of one of the huge towers built by King Herod to protect his palace; it was spared by the Romans in their destruction of Jerusalem in AD 70. The partially reconstructed foundations of a round tower from the Early Arab period (c. AD 700) and masonry from the time of the Crusader occupation reflect subsequent changes in the fortifications of the Citadel. Most of the existing ramparts and vaults, however, were built by the Mamluks in the 13th and 14th centuries. Some additions were made by the Ottoman sultan Suleiman the Magnificent in the 16th century. Among the most conspicuous reminders of the Ottoman period is the Citadel's minaret, built in 1635. Since the 19th century, the name "David's Tower" (Heb. *Migdal David*) has often been applied specifically to this minaret, and it has become one of the best-known symbols of the city of

Night view of the Citadel Museum of the History of Jerusalem

Jerusalem.

Exhibits are located in several interior halls of the complex. In one hall, the story of Jerusalem is told through excavated artifacts, which include catapult stones; bricks bearing the insigne LXF (*Legionis X Fretensis*) of the 10th Roman Legion, which carried out the destruction of the city; medieval arms and armor; and such relatively modern finds as coffee cups and smoking pipes used by Ottoman soldiers in the 19th century.

Model of 19th-century Jerusalem

Throughout the Citadel, well-presented models, maps, charts, and labels clarify its complicated history. Especially appealing is a large three-dimensional model of Jerusalem crafted in zinc by a Hungarian, Stephen Illes, in 1872. The story of its recent rediscovery is told in the label: the 15-by-13-foot model of the Holy City, exhibited by Illes all over Europe in the late 19th century, was eventually forgotten and remained stored in the basement of a Geneva museum until the early 1980s, when it was located and identified by Hebrew University students. Beyond its historical significance, Illes' model is still a useful guide to the topography and geography of Jerusalem.

Focusing on the inhabitants of Jerusalem is a large collection of handmade dolls in typical costumes and poses of the city's many ethnic and religious groups. Each of the dozens of dolls—whether a Yemenite Jew or a Franciscan friar or an Arab peasant (*fallah*)—is fashioned and dressed with faithful attention to detail.

In addition to the exhibits, a multiscreen show, "Shalom Jerusalem," tells of the city's uniqueness and its importance to Judaism, Christianity, and Islam. Nightly (except in the winter months) a Sound and Light presentation in the Citadel's courtyard highlights the main events and personalities of Jerusalem's history in this most appropriate setting.

Both children and adults delight in exploring the Citadel's ramparts, vaults, towers, and moat and find its exhibition halls a means to learning as well as to enjoyment.

FRANCISCAN BIBLICAL MUSEUM

Church of the Flagellation, Second Station
Via Dolorosa, Old City
Jerusalem

HOURS: Mon.–Sat. 9–11:30   TEL.: 02–280271
Sunday by appointment only (groups not to exceed 20 people)   ADMISSION: Free

Focus: **Early Christian Sites**

The Franciscan Biblical Museum is located on the Via Dolorosa—the Way of
Sorrows—the route that, according to tradition, Jesus followed to Golgotha.
Since the defeat of the Crusaders, the Franciscans, as custodians of the holy
places, have been instrumental in guiding Christian pilgrims along this route
and in preserving many other ancient sites sacred to Christendom. This museum continues the centuries-old tradition. Opened in 1902 at the Monastery of

Head of an angel from a fresco in the basilica at Gethsemane

St. Saviour, it was transferred to the present location in 1931. The museum's collections represent the work of Franciscan archaeologists, who have a long record of excavation and research in the Holy Land.

The collections are, for the most part, arranged according to excavation site; most prominent are Nazareth, Capernaum, and the place on Jerusalem's Mount of Olives known as Dominus Flevit ("the Lord wept"), where Jesus "beheld the city and wept over it" (Luke 19:41). Excavations at these sites uncovered many artifacts from the Herodian period, which were of particular interest to the Franciscans in their investigations of the early days of Christianity. Artifacts from later historical periods include the Treasure of Bethlehem; a cache of Crusader liturgical objects, among them many bells and organ pipes, from the Church of the Nativity; and a comprehensive and well-known collection of coins of the Holy Land.

Other aspects of life in the Holy Land are illumined by a charming group of 18th-century jars and containers made in Italy specifically for the pharmacy that the Franciscans operated in Jerusalem and a 17th-century model of the Church of the Holy Sepulchre, made of olive wood and inlaid with mother-of-pearl, a fine example of regional woodcraft.

ISRAEL GOOR THEATER ARCHIVE AND MUSEUM

Mount Scopus Campus, Hebrew University
Jerusalem

HOURS: Mon. and Thurs. 8:30–12

TEL.: 02–883986
ADMISSION: Free

Focus: Documentation of Israeli and Jewish Theater

The Israel Goor Theater Archive and Museum, which moved in 1987 to its present quarters at the Hebrew University campus on Mount Scopus, is international in scope. The collection covers not only the theater in Israel but also the Jewish theater wherever it exists or has existed. Students, scholars, and drama buffs can find here, for example, the scripts of all the plays that have appeared on the Israeli stage. The collection includes a variety of theater posters and memorabilia. Documents and visual materials relating to the Habimah Theater—from the time of its establishment in Moscow, in 1921, to the present—are a valued part of this important collection.

The museum publishes the only Hebrew theater quarterly, *Bamah* (*Stage*), which has been in print for over 50 years. The great usefulness of this museum/archive as a resource for research on the Israeli and the Jewish theater is enhanced by the presence of a knowledgeable and accommodating curator.

GREEK ORTHODOX PATRIARCHATE MUSEUM

Greek Orthodox Patriarchate Street
Christian Quarter, Old City
Jerusalem

HOURS: Mon.–Fri. 9–13 and 15–17, Sat. 9–13

TEL.: 02–284006
ADMISSION: $.50

Focus: Antiquities of the Holy Land

Gathered over the past century, the collection of antiquities housed in this restored 12th-century building of the Crusader period comprises archaeological finds and chance discoveries on properties in and around Jerusalem owned by the Greek Orthodox Church. In addition to the archaeological artifacts, the museum features traditional Greek Orthodox liturgical objects such as manuscripts, embroideries, and ceremonial goblets.

Of special interest are two white stone coffins, or sarcophagi, found about 100 years ago in the so-called Herod's Family Tomb, near the King David Hotel. The identification of this tomb with the royal family has been called in question, but the sarcophagi it contained are among the most elaborate examples of Jewish funerary art of the 1st century BC. Handsomely decorated with floral motifs, they are similar to sarcophagi owned by the Louvre that were found in 1863 in the Tombs of the Kings in northern Jerusalem.

Numerous architectural fragments of the Crusader period are also exhibited; many of these came from the Church of Mary la Grande, which stood near the Holy Sepulchre and was destroyed after the defeat of the Crusaders. Among the figurative pieces are a capital showing a unique medieval hunting scene and another bearing the image of the Virgin Mary. Additional displays include a collection of Roman and Byzantine glass, a group of Late Roman statuettes, and some Early Christian funerary inscriptions carved in stone.

HECHAL HAGVURAH MUSEUM

Russian Compound
Jerusalem

HOURS: Sun.–Thurs. 9–16 (9–15 in winter), Fri. 10–13	TEL.: 02–233209 Admission: $1.50

> *Focus:* **History of Jewish Underground Organizations**

Hechal Hagvurah Museum

Opposite: Photographs of members of the underground executed by the British

The building that houses this museum has had a long and varied history. Built in 1864, it was part of the Russian Compound, one of the first extensive building projects outside the walls of the Old City, and it served as a hostel for Russian women pilgrims to the Holy Land until, with the onset of World War I, the mass pilgrimages from Russia ended. In 1918, after the British conquest of Jerusalem, several buildings of the Russian Compound became vacant and were soon taken over to house the administration of the British Mandate; the former women's hostel was renovated to serve as a high-security prison. This Hall of Heroism memorializes the intense, often violent struggle of Jewish underground organizations in Palestine against the British authorities in a determined attempt to establish an independent Jewish state.

The museum itself, as well as its exhibits, documents the struggle. Opened to the public in 1965, it is maintained by the Underground Prisoners' Association (as is the Museum of Heroism in Acre; see page 201). In the entry hall are enlarged photographs of members of the underground who were executed by the British. In the cells once occupied by prisoners, the history of the Jewish underground in Palestine—from its origins during the Arab riots of 1920, which broke out after the British promised the Jews a "National Home" in Palestine—is depicted through newspaper clippings, letters, and photographs. The career of Ze'ev (Vladimir) Jabotinsky, an early leader of Jewish self-defense who was arrested and tried by the British, is also documented.

A visit to the Hall of Heroism is sobering; visible in one cell are the holes made in the wall when two prisoners blew themselves up on the day they were scheduled to be executed. The gallows on display in another part of the former prison was in fact never used, since the British chose to hang Jewish political prisoners in Acre rather than risk public disturbances in predominantly Jewish Jerusalem. A tunnel through which twelve prisoners escaped in 1948 can still be seen. A memorial tablet lists the operations undertaken against the British by the various Jewish underground organizations: the Haganah (Defense); the Irgun Tzvai Leumi (National Military Organization), also known by its acronym, Etzel; and the Stern Gang.

The exterior of the building bears other traces of its history; carved into the stone is the monogram PP, for "Palestine Police." Also on this former hostel—and on the ecclesiastical buildings of the Russian Compound—are prominent oval reliefs with Cyrillic insignia, the emblem of the Russian Orthodox Church. The buildings of the Russian compound, most of which are not now open to the public, represent an important chapter in Jerusalem's history. Just outside Hechal Hagvurah stands the major structure in the compound, the Cathedral of St. Trinity, built in the 1860s in an elaborate Muscovite Baroque style.

HERZL MUSEUM

Herzl Boulevard
Jerusalem

HOURS: Sun.–Thurs. 9–18:30, Fri. 9–13

TEL.: 02–531108
Admission: Free

> In Basel, I created the Jewish State. Were I to say this, I would be greeted by universal laughter. But perhaps five years hence, in any case, certainly fifty years hence, everyone will perceive it. —*Herzl's diary, 1897*

Theodor Herzl's Vienna study

Opposite: Night view, of Israel Museum with Monastery of the Holy Cross in the foreground

The Herzl Museum is located near the entrance gate to Mount Herzl, on whose summit Theodor Herzl (1860–1904), who conceived the idea of a modern Jewish state, is buried. The museum was opened in 1960 to mark the centennial of Herzl's birth.

The museum's collections document the life of Herzl as man, writer, and Zionist. A central feature is the reconstruction of his Vienna study with its original furnishings. Significant personal memorabilia include pages from Herzl's diaries, his correspondence with Pope Pius X, King Victor Emmanuel III of Italy, and other world leaders, and the first draft of *Altneuland*, the novel, published in 1902, in which Herzl recorded his dream of an independent Jewish state in Palestine.

From Herzl's tomb, at the top of the mount, on a clear day one can see the Mediterranean on the western horizon and the Dead Sea to the east. Between them lies Herzl's vision, his "Old-New Land." The slopes of Mount Herzl are studded with white tombstones marking the graves of soldiers who have lost their lives since 1948 in Israel's wars.

THE ISRAEL MUSEUM

Ruppin Boulevard
Jerusalem

HOURS: Sun., Mon., Wed., Thurs. 10–17, Tues. 16–22, Fri. and Sat. 10–14 Cafeteria serving dairy food	TEL.: 02–698211 ADMISSION: $3.00 ($4.50 including the Shrine of the Book)

Focus: **Archaeology, Judaica, Ethnography, and Fine Arts**

Situated on a hill in western Jerusalem, the Israel Museum overlooks some of the city's best-known landmarks: the Knesset, the Givat Ram campus of the Hebrew University, and the ancient Monastery of the Cross. The museum complex is itself a distinctive element of the Jerusalem landscape; designed by Alfred Mansfield and Dora Gad, it consists of a series of white stone and glass pavilions that cling to the hill in a manner reminiscent of houses in a traditional Mediterranean village.

When the Israel Museum opened, in 1965, it was composed of five major elements: the Bezalel National Art Museum, the first museum to be established in the country (1906); the Samuel Bronfman Biblical and Archaeological Museum; the Shrine of the Book; the Billy Rose Sculpture Garden; and the Ruth Youth Wing. While the main emphases have remained on the history and art of the land of Israel and the Jewish people, the Israel Museum also houses notable collections of Islamic, Western European, Oceanic, African, Asian, North American Indian, and Pre-Columbian art. Its presentation of contemporary art is enriched by exhibits of photography, architecture, and design.

The Israel Museum has become recognized as one of the finest museums in the world, distinguished for the scope of its collections and the beauty and vitality of its presentations. In a country with a population of only about four million, the Israel Museum attracts close to a million visitors per year, an attendance figure rivaling those of far larger museums in Europe and America. As in any major museum, there is much to see and much ground to cover. Especially if time is limited, visitors should probably concentrate first on the treasures unique to the Israel Museum: the Shrine of the Book, the archaeological collection, and the Jewish Heritage exhibitions.

THE SHRINE OF THE BOOK

Focus: **The Dead Sea Scrolls**

Leading into the museum grounds is the Carter Promenade, a series of broad steps lined with olive trees, modern sculptures, and classical statues. Up a few steps and immediately to the right is the Shrine of the Book, the D. Samuel and Jeane H. Gottesman Center for Biblical Manuscripts, which houses one of Israel's greatest national treasures, the Dead Sea Scrolls. Designed by Frederick J. Kiesler and Armand P. Bartos, the Shrine of the Book features a black basalt rectilinear wall facing a large white dome shaped like the lid of one of the jars in which the scrolls were found. The contrast between the white and black forms symbolizes the struggle of good against evil, of light against darkness, one of the central religious themes expressed in the 2,000-year-old Dead Sea Scrolls. The entrance to the Shrine is a darkened, tunnel-like passage reminiscent of the desert caves in which the ancient manuscripts were found.

The story of the discovery of the Dead Sea Scrolls is a dramatic one. In 1947 a Beduin shepherd, pursuing a stray goat into a cave near the shore of the Dead Sea, chanced upon a cache of seven ancient scrolls stored in clay jars (as recommended by Jeremiah [32:13]: "Put them in an earthen vessel that they

The Shrine of the Book

may continue many days"). Four of the scrolls were eventually purchased by the Syrian Orthodox Monastery of Saint Mark in the Old City of Jerusalem; the other three were acquired by Professor Eliezer Sukenik of the Hebrew University on November 29, 1947, the day the United Nations voted to partition Palestine. Sukenik, recognizing that the form of the Hebrew script resembled inscriptions from 2,000-year-old tombs, was the first to realize the enormous significance of the scrolls.

Syrian Orthodox Bishop Mar Athanasius Yeshue Samuel subsequently smuggled the four scrolls out of the country. Sukenik did not live to see the scrolls returned to Jerusalem, but his son Yigael Yadin traveled to America in 1955 and, with the aid of New York philanthropist D. Samuel Gottesman, acquired the scrolls on behalf of the newly established State of Israel.

The scrolls exhibited in the domed gallery of the Shrine of the Book are written on parchment, most of them in Hebrew, a few in Aramaic. They include both biblical and non-biblical writings compiled by an ancient Jewish sect, probably the Essenes, who lived at Qumran, near the northwestern shore of the Dead Sea. This community, whose members led ascetic and contemplative lives, was founded sometime in the 2nd century BC and was destroyed by the Romans during the Great Revolt (AD 67–73). The scrolls on display include the Manual of Discipline, a document detailing the rules that governed the life of the sect; the Scroll of the Sons of Light Against the Sons of Darkness, a description of a final apocalyptic war between the sect and the forces of evil in the world; a commentary on the Book of Habakkuk; the Psalms Scroll, a collection of hymns; part of the Isaiah Scroll; and the Temple Scroll, an idealized, mystical description of Jerusalem (acquired in 1967).

The Dead Sea Scrolls, which include fragments of every book of the Hebrew Bible except the Book of Esther, are by far the oldest known biblical manuscripts. The Isaiah Scroll, for example, is a full thousand years older than any other extant Hebrew biblical text. These documents have given scholars a unique opportunity to study the early development of the Bible and the religious trends in the country in the two centuries before the destruction of the Second Temple by the Romans, in AD 70.

Another group of ancient documents and artifacts exhibited in the Shrine

Interior of the Shrine of the Book

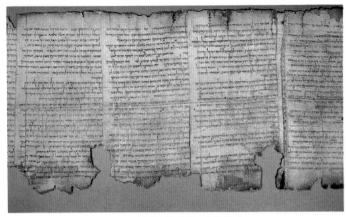

The Isaiah Scroll, Shrine of the Book

of the Book sheds light on some of the personalities and events of the doomed revolt against Rome led by Bar Kokhba in AD 132–35. Found in 1960 in a cave near Ein Gedi (now known as the Cave of Letters) by an archaeological team headed by Professor Yigael Yadin, they apparently belonged to besieged Jewish rebels and refugees. The documents include fifteen letters from Bar Kokhba—military dispatches sent by him to leaders of the revolt in Ein Gedi—which help to lessen the obscurity surrounding the life of this almost legendary figure. A number of papyrus texts, deeds, and certificates written in Hebrew, Aramaic, Greek, and Nabataean—the personal papers of a woman named Babata—offer substantial insights into life in the late 1st and early 2nd century. Baskets, door keys, a skein and balls of wool, textiles, bronze jugs, leatherwork, and an exceptionally beautiful glass plate are among the other finds from the Cave of Letters displayed here.

After leaving the Shrine of the Book, visitors can return to the Carter Promenade and ascend the steps to the Billy Rose Sculpture Garden. Beyond the sculpture garden is the plaza in front of the main entrance to the museum.

THE BILLY ROSE SCULPTURE GARDEN

Highlights: **Auguste Rodin, *Adam*; Henry Moore, *Vertebrae*; Robert Indiana, *Ahava (Love)***

Set in the midst of a rocky Jerusalem landscape, this sculpture garden, designed by Isamu Noguchi, consists of a series of semicircular graveled terraces enclosed by stone retaining walls. Currently over fifty major sculptures, most of which were donated by the American stage and film impresario Billy Rose, occupy this outdoor exhibition area. Highlighted against the stark background of the surrounding Judean Hills are works of Robert Indiana, Jacques Lipchitz, Aristide Maillol, Henry Moore, Elie Nadelman, Pablo Picasso, and Auguste Rodin—to mention but a few—as well as of Israeli sculptors Yitzhak Danziger, Benni Ephrat, Michael Gross, Menashe Kadishman, David Palombo, and Igael Tumarkin.

Adjoining the Billy Rose Sculpture Garden is the Jacques Lipchitz Pavilion, containing that artist's sketches and a few other small-scale sculptures. The Billy Rose Pavilion also features exhibitions of sculpture, with emphasis on the avant-garde.

THE MAIN BUILDING

The spacious plaza in front of the main entrance to the museum presents an unexpected contrast of artistic styles and periods: black basalt gables from a 3rd-century Galilean synagogue, a Roman marble frieze from Caesarea, and temporary exhibits of modern sculpture. On the facing hills, an urban collage of 19th- and 20th-century neighborhoods forms an equally dramatic backdrop. The understated entrance to the main building of the museum is located at the left end of the building's dark-glass facade. Inside, on the entry level, to the left, is the museum gift shop. To the right are several galleries utilized for special exhibitions.

THE SAMUEL BRONFMAN BIBLICAL AND ARCHAEOLOGICAL MUSEUM

Highlights: **The Judean Desert Treasure; Shrine of the Stelae from Hazor; Anthropoid Coffins; Amulets with Priestly Benediction; Bronze Torso of the Emperor Hadrian**

Located to the left of the staircase that descends from the entrance hall, the Bronfman galleries contain rich archaeological collections illustrating the history of the land of Israel from prehistoric times to the Middle Ages. The exhibits, which include some of the most important finds from scientific excavations throughout Israel, are arranged chronologically.

Although the cultural remains of the land of Israel lack the splendor of Egyptian art or the majesty of Mesopotamian architecture, they reflect a vibrant interchange of the ideas and styles of many peoples of the ancient world.

Billy Rose Sculpture Garden

*Ivory statuettes
from Be'er Sheva,
end of
5th millennium BC*

As a strategic crossroads for the armies of mighty neighbors and as a major conduit of international trade, the land of the Bible was the birthplace of religious and cultural concepts that profoundly influenced the development of the Western world. The artifacts exhibited here illuminate the country's culture and artistic achievements throughout its history; because of their connection with the Bible their effect is particularly forceful. Text panels, charts, and maps offer valuable historical background, and the exhibits themselves are visually enhanced by huge photomurals of sites and landscapes.

Beginning with the Paleolithic period, displays of skeletal remains, tools, and other finds illustrate the development of early humans as hunters and food-gatherers. Stirrings of the impulse toward artistic and perhaps religious expression can be seen in stone figurines and animals carved of bone from the 9th millennium BC. Artifacts from the succeeding period, the Neolithic, include the earliest agricultural implements and fired clay vessels—signs of the start of a settled, farming way of life. Near-life-size clay effigies and ceremonial masks, some of stone—also from the Neolithic period—give a sense of the elaborateness of early religious ritual.

The first evidence of smelting and metalworking can be seen in finds from the Chalcolithic period. The most spectacular remains from this period—and indeed in the history of archaeology in Israel—is the Judean Desert Treasure, found in 1961 in a cave at Nahal Mishmar, near Ein Gedi, by a team headed by Pessach Bar Adon. This cache consists of 429 artifacts, most of them cast in copper. Apparently religious or ceremonial in intent, they include "crowns" (one decorated with birds and animals), jars, scepters, maces,

Anthropoid clay coffins, 12th century BC

and dozens of individual maceheads. The level of the culture in the Negev in this period is indicated by two remarkably expressive clay cultic vessels from Gilat, one in the form of a ram with three jars on its back and the other in the form of a seated nude woman or goddess holding a large churn on her head. Male and female ivory statuettes from the Be'er Sheva area also attest to a high artistic standard. Unique Chalcolithic burial customs are reflected in small round or house-shaped coffins, or ossuaries, used for the deposit of the bones of the deceased.

In successive halls are displayed finds from the Canaanite period (Bronze Age) representing the cultures of its early, middle, and late phases. The development of writing and the impact of contemporaneous civilizations in Egypt and Mesopotamia can be followed in the material culture of Canaan. Egyptian-style scarabs and Mesopotamian-style cylinder seals, pottery imported from Cyprus and Mycenaean Greece, Egyptian-style faience and alabaster vessels, as well as luxury wares made locally, are among the exhibits. Outstanding evidences of Canaanite religious practices are cult objects, including a mold for a figurine of Astarte, from a sanctuary of the 17th century BC near Nahariya, and the 14th–13th-century Shrine of the Stelae from Hazor, with its carved images of a seated man and a lion and its series of small basalt stelae, one of which shows two hands raised in prayer toward a crescent moon. A nearby staircase leads to the Braumiller Gallery, where additional Canaanite religious and cultic objects are displayed.

In the last three centuries of the Canaanite period, the Egyptian New Kingdom dominated Canaan, and the pervasive Egyptian influence can be seen in a group of large clay anthropoid coffins, shaped like mummy cases, each bearing a stylized portrait of the deceased. Also shown is a wide array of jewelry, scarab seals, bronze vessels, and other luxury objects—many of them imported—found with and inside the coffins at the site of Deir el-Balah, south of Gaza.

Finds from the Israelite period illuminate the biblical account of the settlement and unification of the Israelite tribes and the establishment of the Judean and Israelite monarchies. During that period, the Philistines, one of the Aegean Sea Peoples, played an important cultural and political role. "Ashdoda," a goddess-and-chair figurine from Ashdod, and a group of clay vessels with colorful decorations uncovered at Philistine temples in Tell Qasile (see also Eretz Israel Museum, page 90) demonstrate the vitality of the Philistine culture. The lingering influence of Canaanite religious traditions is also evidenced by the cultic stands and fertility figurines, all of which were found on Israelite sites.

Among the royal remains from this period are a stone balustrade from a Judean palace-fortress, beautifully carved ivories from the Israelite palace in Samaria, and a proto-Ionic capital from a gateway built by King Ahab in Hazor. Especially noteworthy is the reassembled Holy of Holies from Arad, a Judean royal fortress and administrative center in the Negev. Its shrine consists of two incense altars, a stone stele, and a raised platform—elements also contained in the Holy of Holies in the Temple in Jerusalem (I Kings 6:16).

The Judean and Israelite monarchies were both overcome at the end of the Iron Age with the rise of great neighboring empires; the exhibited artifacts from the 7th and 6th centuries BC evoke the conquests of the invaders who swept over the two kingdoms. Finds from the Judean city of Lachish, conquered in 701 BC by Sennacherib, are displayed near the clay prism describing the Assyrian king's victories over the cities of King Hezekiah of Judah. Extending along the wall is a plaster cast of a huge relief from Sennacherib's palace depicting the siege of Lachish. In 586 BC, Lachish was conquered once again, this time by Nebuchadnezzar, ruler of the Babylonian empire. As the text panels recount, it was in the same year that he destroyed Jerusalem, that "he burnt the House of the Lord, and the king's house, and all the houses of Jerusalem . . . ." (II Kings 25:9). This marked the end of the Israelite period and the beginning of the Babylonian Exile.

A series of steps lead to the displays from the succeeding Persian period, during which the Persian king Cyrus permitted the Jews to return to their land and to rebuild the Temple, as recounted in the Book of Ezra and the Book of Nehemiah. The period is relatively poor in material produced locally, but the many luxury goods imported into the country at this time include painted Greek vases, Persian gold jewelry, and Phoenician glass pendants.

Just off the main galleries, two special galleries are devoted, respectively, to the development of ancient glass and of the Hebrew script. The exhibit of glass and glassmaking spans over 3,500 years, ranging from the earliest opaque glass vessels made in Egypt and Mesopotamia to the blown-glass utensils and vessels of Roman and Byzantine times. Especially beautiful are the ancient vessels covered with a silvery patina, a phenomenon of weathering and aging.

In the adjacent gallery, the Hecht Pavilion of Hebrew Script and Inscriptions, ancient seals, coins, ostraca, jar handles, inscribed jars, and casts of monumental inscriptions tell the story of the alphabet and illustrate how writing was used in ritual, in art, and in everyday life. A chart shows the evolution of the ancient Hebrew 22-letter alphabet from the proto-Canaanite pictographic characters of the 18th century BC, and explains how Greek, Latin, Arabic, and other alphabets were developed from it. Coins, seals, and the often tiny inscriptions on display are accompanied by enlarged drawings and by extensive explanatory texts that provide translations and additional information. Among the highlights are two small silver scrolls, used as amulets, found in Jerusalem burial caves of the 7th century BC. The text they bear is almost identical to the priestly benediction in the Book of Numbers (6:24–26).

The chronological exhibits continue with finds dating from the Hellenistic, Roman, and Byzantine periods, covering events from the conquest of the land by Alexander the Great in 332 BC to the Muslim conquest in AD 640. The first phase of this era—the late Second Temple period—witnessed the rise of an independent Judean kingdom founded by the Maccabees (also known as the Hasmoneans) in 165 BC, and the monumental public building projects of Herod the Great, including the enlargement of the Temple in Jerusalem, the construction of the opulent winter palace-fortress at Masada, and the establishment of the port city of Caesarea.

This was a time of great importance for the future of Western civilization, since it saw the beginnings of Christianity. Especially evocative in this connection is a Latin inscription on a fragment of a limestone block from Caesarea—the name and title of Pontius Pilate, the procurator of Judea (AD 26–36) under whose rule the crucifixion of Jesus took place.

From the city of Jerusalem comes a Hebrew inscription carved in a huge block of stone that was excavated at a lower level of the southwestern corner of the Temple Mount. It reads "To the place of trumpeting"—a vivid confirmation of the description by the Jewish historian Josephus of the weekly blowing of a trumpet by a priest standing on top of the priests' chamber in the Temple, to announce the coming of the Sabbath. Other important remains from this period excavated in the Jewish Quarter in recent years, including mosaic floors, stone utensils, decorated pottery, and glass vessels, shed light on life in

Jerusalem during the last days before the destruction of the city by the Romans in AD 70. A monumental Corinthian capital suggests the elaborateness of the architecture in the city in the late Second Temple period.

The Roman gallery covers the period from the destruction of Jerusalem to AD 324, when Constantine became the sole ruler of the Roman Empire and his support of Christianity transformed Palestina (as it was known in Latin) into an important province and a place of pilgrimage for the entire empire. The exhibits here are dominated by an exceptional larger-than-life bronze torso of the emperor Hadrian, discovered at the site of a legionary encampment near Beit She'an. Several other examples of Roman metalwork are shown, among them a bronze head of a youth and an iron parade helmet. Statuary of the Roman period includes a marble griffin with a paw resting on the wheel of fate of the goddess Nemesis, found in the Negev, and a fragmentary statue of Artemis of Ephesus, found in Caesarea.

Many fine mosaics belong to the following period, the Byzantine, when Christian pilgrimage increased and major church construction took place. Synagogues of both the Roman and the Byzantine period are also represented: mosaics and architectural elements testify to the survival and development of Palestinian Jewry during that time, in which the laws and legal interpretations of the Mishna and Talmud were codified.

The pottery, glass, jewelry, coins, and architectural fragments exhibited in the next gallery cover the cultural history of the land from the Muslim conquest, completed in 640, to the Crusader Kingdom of the 12th–13th century.

The last gallery in the archaeological collections provides an overview of the cultures of the neighboring countries that most strongly influenced the land and people of Israel in antiquity. Finds from Mesopotamia include cuneiform tablets, cylinder seals, inscriptions, bronze figurines, wall reliefs, and mud bricks, one bearing the seal of Sargon II, who conquered the Kingdom of Israel, and another with the seal of Nebuchadnezzar, who destroyed Jerusalem in 586 BC. These artifacts span the periods from the earliest kingdoms of Sumer, in the 4th millennium BC, through the Babylonian empire of the 7th–6th century BC. The cultural sophistication of Egypt is apparent in several 14th-century BC stone reliefs from Amarna and a selection of scarabs and amulets. Artifacts from Iran (ancient Persia) include early painted pottery and some of the fine metalwork for which Luristan, in the northwest, was famous. In this gallery representing neighboring cultures there are also pottery from tombs of the Early Bronze Age in Cyprus, some Cypro-Phoenician vessels, and both pottery and metalwork from Anatolia (modern Turkey). A collection of Greek painted vases of the classical period is exhibited on a small balcony.

Bird's Head Haggadah, Rhineland, c. 1300

THE JEWISH HERITAGE EXHIBITIONS

Highlights: **Wall of Hanukkah Lamps; The Vittorio Veneto and Horb Synagogues; Bird's Head Haggadah (c. 1300); Moroccan Room**

A brief video program, well worth watching, introduces the visitor to the Jewish Heritage collection, its origins and its significance.

The collection of Judaica in the Israel Museum is among the finest in the world. The small nucleus assembled at Bezalel, the country's first art museum, established in 1906, has grown steadily into a comprehensive collection of Jewish ceremonial art and artifacts reflecting the traditions of the Jewish people from antiquity to modern times as observed in Jewish communities all over the world. Examples of the craftsmanship and art of both major traditions, the Sephardi and the Ashkenazi, are represented. The Sephardim originated in Spain (Heb. *Sepharad*), but the term has come to embrace the Jews of North Africa and the Middle East as well; the Ashkenazim came from Germany (*Ashkenaz*, in medieval Hebrew), but the term has come to embrace the Jews of Central, Eastern, and Northern Europe.

Despite regional differences, Jews all over the world share a large body of rituals and festival customs. Fundamental to the practice of Judaism is the Torah—the first five books of the Bible, or the Pentateuch—on which the religious and legal principles of Judaism are based. The scrolls of the Torah, kept in the synagogue, are objects of profound veneration, and over the centuries their sanctity has inspired flights of artistic creativity in the design of decorative accessories. Usually in Sephardi communities the Torah scrolls are protected by decorative wooden or silver containers, while Ashkenazim wrap them in embroidered covers. Equally expressive of reverence are the ornate silver plaque, or breastplate (Heb. *tas*), that is hung over the Torah cover and the finials or crowns that adorn the handles of the staves on which the scrolls are rolled. With their wealth of decorative elements, elaborate designs, and ingenious arrangements, they are a stirring legacy from the craftsmen of Germany, Poland, Italy, Turkey, Afghanistan, Morocco, and Yemen, many of them unnamed. Fine examples of embroidered *parochot*, Torah Ark curtains, are also on display.

The observance of the Sabbath is another universal element in Jewish life, and the sanctity of the Day of Rest is brought to mind by many other objects in the collections: goblets for the wine over which the *kiddush* ("sanctification")—the ceremonial blessing—is recited; candlesticks and oil lamps for the lights that are kindled on Friday evening at sundown; covers for the *hallah*, the Sabbath loaf; special Sabbath tablecloths; and a wonderfully diverse selection of spice boxes, used in the *havdalah* ceremony at the close of the Sabbath, marking its separation from the ordinary days of the week. Many of these spice boxes, inspired by the architecture of the European cities where they were fashioned, are shaped like medieval towers; others are created in imaginative forms such as flowers, fruits, and fish, and there is even a miniature steam locomotive.

A major portion of Jewish ceremonial art celebrates the cycle of the Jewish year, and the Judaica galleries amply represent the variety and beauty of the artifacts connected with the festivals. The cycle begins with Rosh Hashanah, the New Year, followed, ten days later, by Yom Kippur, the Day of Atonement. The rams's horn, or *shofar*, that is sounded in synagogues all over the world is shown here in some of its most interesting variations, and here too are special garments worn on the high holy days. Sukkot, the autumn Festival of Tabernacles—observed by "dwelling," or at least holding festive meals, in a *sukkah*, a temporary "booth" decorated with plants, fruits, and vegetables symbolizing the bounty of the harvest—is represented by a rare reconstructed 19th-century *sukkah* from southern Germany with idealized landscapes of Jerusalem painted on its interior walls. Another decorative feature of traditional *sukkot* are pictures of heroes of biblical history, called *ushpizin*. One especially beautiful example is a lacelike parchment cutout, colored in tempera paint, depicting Aaron and Moses. Also associated with the Festival of Tabernacles are cases for the *etrog*, or citron, one of the "Four Species" (the others being palm, willow, and myrtle) used in the synagogue and the home. Silver, glass, wood, and brass are the materials of the *etrog* cases shown here, many of them wonderfully crafted.

The next major holiday, Hanukkah, or the Festival of Lights, celebrates the victory of the Maccabees over the Syrian Greeks in 165 BC and the reconsecration of the defiled Temple in Jerusalem. In remembrance of the miracle of a single jar of oil that burned for eight days, Jewish families traditionally light candles in a special eight-branched lamp, the menorah or *hanukkiah*. The Israel Museum's impressive collection of these lamps—including one of cast bronze made in Spain or southern France in the 14th century and an unusual one made of limestone in 19th-century Palestine—encompasses many different styles, materials, and places of origin and reflects the continuing prominence of this ceremonial object throughout the Diaspora.

The religious observance of the spring festivals of Purim and Passover are also highlighted in the Jewish Heritage collections. Among the items connected with Purim celebrations are illuminated *megillot*—scrolls of the Book of Esther—and children's noisemakers, or *groggers*. Centering on Passover are ceremonial plates for the symbolic foods, including a rare 15th-century lusterware plate from Spain, goblets, and other objects used during the Seder service.

Many of the objects exhibited are connected with ceremonies performed during the Jewish life cycle, from birth to death—from circumcision and the "redeeming" of the firstborn son, to marriage, to burial. Illuminated *ketubbot* (wedding contracts) from throughout the Diaspora illustrate both the similarities and the differences between communities. Some of the *ketubbot*, especially those from Italy, are very ornate and approach high art, while other, cruder examples are typical of folk art.

In the realm of folk art, the wide-ranging collections include amulets designed to provide protection from evils such as sickness, some inscribed with mystical Hebrew texts. A characteristic good-luck charm of Sephardi communities is an amulet shaped like a hand, called a *hamsa* from the Arabic word for "five." Other noteworthy examples of Jewish folk art are paper cutouts, calendars, and the *mizrah* and *shiviti*—panels traditionally hung in the home or synagogue to indicate the proper direction of prayer, toward Jerusalem.

Not to be missed is the exhibit of rare Jewish manuscripts, including the DeCastro Pentateuch, from Germany, dated 1344, and the Rothschild Miscellany, from Italy, written and illuminated on parchment in 1470. The 949 pages of the latter, with colored illustrations, contain nearly 50 separate religious and literary works. Another remarkable manuscript is the Bird's Head Haggadah, written about 1300 in the Rhineland; its bird-headed figures conform with the biblical injunction against depicting the human form. The *me-*

zuzah—the small case, containing a parchment scroll with verses from Deuteronomy, that Jews traditionally affix to the doorposts of their homes— is well represented in all its multiplicity of forms and provenances.

Off the main galleries devoted to the Jewish Heritage collections are two unique reconstructed synagogues. On the right is the synagogue from Vittorio Veneto in northern Italy, near Venice, built in 1701. Its baroque interior, featuring carved wooden prayer benches, latticed balconies for the women's section, a wooden *bimah*, or platform, and an ornate gilded Ark of the Law, was dismantled and brought to the Israel Museum in 1964. From Horb, in southern Germany, came a small wooden synagogue whose barrel-vaulted ceiling was painted in 1735 by Eliezer Susmann of Poland with real and

Moroccan Room

mythological animals, trailing vines with fruits, Hebrew inscriptions, and two heraldic lions blowing trumpets. Hundreds of similar small wooden synagogues built in villages and towns throughout Eastern Europe were destroyed during the Holocaust. An earlier example of synagogue decoration can be seen in the two large carved wooden doors of the Fustat synagogue in Cairo, a place of worship renowned throughout the Jewish world as early as the 12th century.

A highlight of the museum's Jewish Heritage section is a collection of some 10,000 ethnographic artifacts, including examples of formal and ordinary dress, jewelry, and everyday objects used in Jewish communities in such widely dispersed locales as Bukhara, Kurdistan, Turkey, Yemen, North Africa, and Eastern Europe. Featured are typical examples of embroidery, handwoven rugs, tie-dyed silks, fur-trimmed hats, men's coats, and women's dresses. Of special interest are the splendid embroidered and brocaded bridal gowns. Several model rooms depict the life-styles of both Ashkenazi and Sephardi communities.

CULTURES OF OTHER LANDS

The Asian Department features exhibits that include ceramics from China, Korea, and Thailand, and Indian paintings, bronzes, and sculptures.

The Pavilion of Ethnic Art offers a glimpse of cultures from across the world. It contains rich collections of American Indian and Pacific arts and crafts, including masks, wood carvings, ceremonial objects, weapons, and shields.

A major gallery is devoted to Pre-Columbian Art, displaying ancient ceramics and metalwork from the empires of South and Central America. Well represented are Inca funerary objects; among these is a rare gold burial mask dating from about AD 1400.

NUMISMATIC GALLERY

Focus: **History of Local Currency**

This small but important gallery surveys the history of coins from its beginnings to the present, with emphasis on the coins used in the land of Israel under its various rulers and governments.

Photomurals illustrate the process of striking coins, which originated during the 7th century BC in the Greek cities of Lydia and Ephesus in Asia Minor. Drawings and text panels enhance the displays of ancient coins and of Jewish medals and commemorative medallions. Two of the highlights are a coin issued by the Romans after AD 73, which bears the image of a woman weeping under a palm tree and the legend "Judea Capta," and a coin issued by the rebels during the time of the Bar Kokhba Revolt (AD 132–35), which shows the facade of the Second Temple.

PERIOD ROOMS

Several European period rooms provide examples of classic French, Italian, and English interior design. Of the two rooms from France, one is decorated in the Empire style, popular in the Napoleonic era and during the first decades of the 19th century; many of the handsome china pieces displayed in it were made in Sèvres. The other is a room originally built for Samuel Bernard, Comte de Coubet, in the 1740s and later dismantled and installed in the house of Baron Edmond de Rothschild in Paris. It was brought to Jerusalem in 1968 as a gift to the Israel Museum from the Rothschild family. The white-and-gilt panels, moldings, and chandeliers are in the Rococo style.

An Italian art pavilion from Venice is decorated in the characteristic chinoiserie style of the 18th century. Paintings by several Italian masters of the 17th and 18th centuries can also be seen here.

An 18th-century paneled English dining room contains period furniture, porcelain, and paintings, in addition to an impressive array of 18th-century silver.

Gallery of Impressionist Art

FINE ARTS

***Highlights*: 20th-Century Israeli Art**

The fine arts collections of the Israel Museum span the period from the 17th century to the present. In a gallery devoted to the Old Masters, visitors can view Dutch and Flemish paintings. In the adjacent galleries the exhibited works represent a wide range, from Pre-Raphaelite to Realist. Among them are a highly romantic view of Jerusalem by Edward Lear and a series of bronze busts by Honoré Daumier caricaturing political figures. Paintings by the 19th-century Jewish artists Maurycy Gottlieb, Josef Israels, and Moritz Oppenheim are also on view. A small collection of paintings and sculptures by Impressionists and Post-Impressionists and their precursors, including Corot, Degas, Monet, Pissarro, Renoir, Van Gogh, and Rodin, is displayed effectively in a gallery illuminated by natural light. Works by 20th-century artists such as Utrillo, Matisse, Chagall, and Kokoschka are also shown here. Temporary exhibits periodically draw upon the museum's growing collection of contemporary European and American art, from Cubist to Post-Conceptual.

Contemporary Israeli art has a permanent place in the Israel Museum in the Ayala Zacks-Abramov Pavilion and the Merzbacher Galleries. Oversize walls enhance the presentations from the museum's wide-ranging collections of paintings and sculptures by 20th-century Israeli artists. Among the pioneers of modern art in Israel whose works are exhibited here are Bezalel (Boris) Schatz and Abel Pann, of the turn of the century; from the 1920s come the distinctly modern motifs of Reuven Rubin and Sionah Tager. Israeli art in the following two decades was deeply influenced by Jewish artists who emigrated from Germany and by others who had studied in Paris. "New Horizons"—the abstract style that gained strength after World War II—is well represented, with works by Avigdor Stematsky, Yehezkel Streichman, and Yosef Zaritsky. The collection continues to place emphasis on the works of avant-garde artists in Israel, and temporary exhibitions can be expected to reflect the latest developments on the Israeli art scene.

A separate 20th-century art pavilion has greatly expanded display space and study areas. It houses the museum's important collections of contemporary prints, drawings, and photographs.

THE RUTH YOUTH WING

Focus: **Art for and by Youngsters**

No visit to the Israel Museum would be complete without a stop at the Ruth Youth Wing, where every day hundreds of schoolchildren from all over the country participate in a wide range of artistic and educational activities. Regarded as one of the finest youth centers in the museum world, it offers youngsters a variety of experiences, including exhibits, meetings and workshops with local artists, and, best of all, abundant opportunities to create their own art. The Youth Wing features such diverse themes as "Ancient Egyptian Art," "The Earth as the Raw Material of the Artist," and "How to Look at a Sculpture." The founder of the Youth Wing and its director since its opening, in 1965, Ayala Gordon, works on the principle that in order to appreciate art, children must be encouraged to express their own creativity. Because of its scope and its relevance, the Youth Wing attracts adults as well as children.

An important adjunct to the Youth Wing, the Mili Center, both provides Israeli teachers with the material and enables them to acquire the know-how to prepare their students for visits to the museum and to help them understand how they can benefit from the remarkable facilities of the institution.

Perhaps the most important contribution of the Youth Wing has been its success in interesting Israeli youngsters in the Israel Museum's vast collections and in encouraging them to bring their families with them during school vacations and holidays. In a country with as diverse a population as Israel—some of it originating in countries where museums barely exist—the opening up of the world of art and culture to schoolchildren has had a wide-ranging positive effect.

In addition to the displays in its capacious exhibition halls, the museum has an extensive library and an outstanding collection of prints and drawings, both open to the public by appointment. It also offers films, lectures, music, and dance programs.

The Israel Museum owes its existence to the initiative of Jerusalem's mayor, Teddy Kollek, who first recognized the need for such an institution, in the 1950s. Kollek realized that none of Jerusalem's then few and modest museums had the prestige or international standing to attract donations of important collections from abroad. Only a truly national museum, he believed, would enable Israel to acquire such collections, as well as to display the country's archaeological treasures adequately. He enlisted the support and cooperation of Mordechai Narkiss, director of the Bezalel National Art Museum, and archaeologists Benjamin Mazar and Yigael Yadin of the Hebrew University in laying the groundwork for the establishment of a multicultural museum, a national center for the arts and antiquities, where Israelis could study their own and other cultures. In its many facets and its many faces, the Israel Museum has probably gone beyond even Mayor Teddy Kollek's dreams.

EDWARD AND HELEN MARDIGIAN MUSEUM

Street of the Armenian Orthodox Patriarchate
Armenian Quarter, Old City
Jerusalem

HOURS: Mon.–Sat. 10–16

TEL.: 02–282331
ADMISSION: $.75

Focus: Armenian History and Culture

Courtyard of the Edward and Helen Mardigian Museum

The Edward and Helen Mardigian Museum, which opened in 1979, is located in the heart of the Armenian Quarter in the Old City. Nearby are the Cathedral of St. James and the residence of the Armenian Patriarch, which form the spiritual center of Jerusalem's Armenian community, one of the oldest outside Armenia. The first Armenians may have come to Jerusalem in the 1st century AD as troops serving in the Roman army. After the conversion of the Armenian nation to Christianity, about the middle of the 3rd century, a significant Armenian community was established in Jerusalem, and it continued to flourish throughout the Byzantine period, when thousands of pilgrims came annually to the Holy City. Currently about 2,000 Armenians live in Jerusalem.

The two-story structure that houses the museum, built in 1843, was originally a theological seminary; its many former cells and public rooms serve as galleries. With its central arcaded courtyard, it is architecturally similar to many local monasteries.

The oldest items on display are fragments of frescoes from the 1st century AD, unearthed nearby on Mount Zion, in the courtyard of the House of Caiaphas, and mosaics from Armenian churches built in the Byzantine period, excavated on Mount Zion and near Damascus Gate.

Interior of Cathedral of St. James. Armenian, 12th century

The Last Supper, *Armenian tile in Cathedral of St. James*

The largest and most important collection consists of precious ritual objects, offerings to the church from pious Armenian pilgrims: liturgical vestments, miters, staffs, and illuminated manuscripts, mostly from the 17th, 18th, and 19th centuries. Other reminders of these many devout pilgrims are a group of huge copper pots used to prepare food for them. More aesthetic in its appeal is the painted ceramic ware for which the Armenians of Jerusalem are famous; a selection of this locally made ware is on display.

Interesting documentary material on view includes letters and records dealing with the Patriarchate's relations with other religious communities in Jerusalem and with Turkish authorities during the period of Ottoman rule. There are also early books and pamphlets printed on Jerusalem's first press, established by the Armenians in 1833.

Some of the first photographs taken in and of Jerusalem are to be seen here; they are the work of Yessayi Gaberdian, who set up his studio in the 1850s. Among the other photographs are scenes of the Armenian homeland, including legendary Mount Ararat, and pictures of some of its present-day inhabitants. A haunting exhibit shows the slaughter and mass starvation of Armenians that occurred in Turkey at the beginning of World War I.

A visit to the Mardigian Museum is no less informative for the fact that it is necessary to wander through many rooms to see all the exhibits.

L. A. MAYER MEMORIAL INSTITUTE FOR ISLAMIC ART

2 Hapalmach Street
Jerusalem

HOURS: Sun.–Thurs. 10–13 and 15:30–18, Sat. 10–13

TEL.: 02–661291
ADMISSION: $2.00

Focus: Art and Crafts of the Islamic World

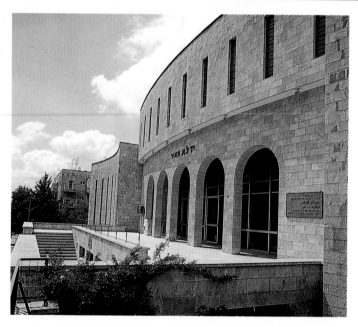

Founded in 1973 as a memorial to the illustrious Israeli Orientalist Leo Ary Mayer (1895–1959), the Institute was the inspiration of the late Vera Brice-Salomons of London, who sought to promote within the Israeli public an appreciation of the artistic achievements of the country's Muslim neighbors.

Entrance into the Institute's attractive galleries is gained through a tall arcade—a stylized adaptation of a traditional Islamic architectural motif—of rose-red stone. The collections, which trace the development of Islamic art from its origins in the 7th century AD, include approximately 5,000 artifacts from Egypt, Syria, Turkey, Iraq, Iran, and India.

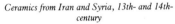

Ceramics from Iran and Syria, 13th- and 14th-century

Turkish 16th- and 17th-century ceramics

Among the elaborately wrought examples of Islamic artistry and craftsmanship are handwoven silk prayer rugs, glassware, jewelry, metalwork, miniatures, and illuminated manuscripts. The abundance of Arabic calligraphy makes it possible to see, for example, a manuscript in Kufic script from 12th-century Iran, a manuscript in Najkhi script from 14th-century Egypt, 18th- and 19th-century Turkish firmans (sultans' edicts), and pages of the Koran from all over the Muslim world.

A group of chess pieces—mostly in ivory, some in jet—from 8th–10th-century Iran bespeak the Middle Eastern origins of the game. (The term "checkmate" derives from the Persian *shah mat*, meaning "The king is dead.")

Ceramic art is prominent among the collections; the lavishly decorated pieces include bowls, basins, canisters, cups, ewers, juglets, platters, vases, tiles, and figurines. Depicted on a 10th-century dish from Nishpur is a voluptuous figure of a dancer traced in yellow slip under a clear glaze. Of special note are groups of ceramic incense vessels in a variety of shapes.

The exhibits stress the development of production methods, such as weaving, dyeing, and glazing, as well as the reciprocal artistic influences of East and West. Informative labels and text panels in Hebrew, Arabic, and English are extensive. The L. A. Mayer Memorial Institute for Islamic Art also houses a comprehensive archive and research library, as well as a photographic collection devoted to Islamic art and architecture. Access to these facilities can be arranged by appointment.

MONASTERY OF THE HOLY CROSS

Valley of the Cross
Haim Hazaz Avenue
Jerusalem

HOURS: Mon.–Thurs. 9–17, Fri. 9–13:30, Sat. 9–17

TEL.: 02–667121
ADMISSION: $1.00

Focus: 11th-Century Ecclesiastical Architecture; Monastic Life

The Monastery of the Holy Cross stands on the site where, according to tradition, the tree grew from whose wood the Holy Cross was made. Its architecture and artworks span centuries of Christian monastic life in Jerusalem. The present monastery, with its buttressed walls, was founded by the Georgian king Bagrat about AD 1050, and it was occupied by Georgian priests throughout the Middle Ages and well into the Ottoman period. Eventually taken over by the Greek Orthodox Church, it was used as a seminary—reputedly one of the finest in the entire Orthodox Christian world—until it was closed, just before the outbreak of World War I. The ornate clock tower was added in the 19th century.

The fortress-like building is entered through a small gateway, the monastery's only connection with the outside world, beyond which lie a series of courtyards planted with a variety of fruit trees. The 11th-century church is built in the authentic Byzantine tradition: a basilica with a central dome supported by six piers. The mosaic floor is unadorned except in its eastern section, where there is a pattern of birds and diamond-shaped medallions. The frescoes, featuring a strange mingling of Greek gods and philosophers and

Christian saints, are from 1643, the year in which the monastery was extensively renovated. To the right of the altar are the remains of a mosaic floor from the late-5th- or early-6th-century church which had stood here. That original church was probably damaged in the Persian invasion of 614 and again in 1009 by order of Caliph el-Hakim.

On the upper floors of the monastery, visitors can view the priests' cells, study rooms, library, and communal dining hall, and also the kitchen, with its ovens and huge cooking vessels. A small museum, on the third floor, displays an odd assortment of artifacts, including photographs of the seminary's graduates, elegant blue-and-white Chinese "export" porcelain platters, a late-17th-century telescope from Paris, a few ancient oil lamps, and some Jewish ossuaries from the 1st century AD. There is also an interesting oil painting on wood depicting the walls and gates of Jerusalem and various episodes in the life of Jesus.

An interesting example of ecclesiastical architecture, the Monastery of the Holy Cross offers a unique glimpse of monastery life of the past.

MUSEUM FOR ISLAMIC ART

**El-Aqsa Mosque
Temple Mount, Old City
Jerusalem**

HOURS: Sat.–Thurs. 8–16 (month of Ramadan 9–11)   TEL.: 02–283313
ADMISSION: $3.50

Focus: Architectural Elements and Ceremonial Art

Located next to el-Aqsa Mosque, the Museum for Islamic Art occupies a building constructed in the 12th century by the Crusader conquerors of Jerusalem. The main structures on the Temple Mount—known in Arabic as Haram esh-Sharif (Noble Sanctuary)—date from the late 7th and early 8th century, yet traces of Crusader architecture are visible throughout the compound, even on the facade of el-Aqsa. This museum, dedicated to the artistic traditions and the craftsmanship of Islam, was opened in 1923, during the British Mandate period. It has undergone extensive renovation and restoration in recent years.

In the entrance hall, ceremonial vessels and other items customarily used in the mosque are exhibited. Of special note is the elaborately decorated gold-and-enamel glass lamp from el-Halil Mosque at the Tombs of the Patriarchs in

Architectural elements in the foreground and el-Aqsa Mosque in the background

Hebron. Also on display are ornate brass candlesticks and incense burners. The work of Islamic armorers is seen in a collection of weapons, swords, sabers, and guns. A section is devoted to illuminated manuscripts and Korans and other books in various styles of Arabic calligraphy. The earliest Koran exhibited here is from the 8th or 9th century and is said to have been written by Muhammad's great-grandson, Ali Muhammad ibn Hasan.

The museum's main hall contains many interesting architectural elements removed from the Dome of the Rock and especially from el-Aqsa in the course of repairs and renovations over the centuries. From the 8th century are fine Umayyad stucco- and stonework, carved wooden beams decorated with floral and geometric designs, and two moon finials from the original mosque. From a later period are an ornamental iron fence placed by the Crusaders around the sacred rock within the Dome of the Rock and six wood-and-bronze doors commissioned for the Dome of the Rock in 1564 by the Turkish sultan Suleiman the Magnificent. The column capitals outside the main entrance of the museum were removed from el-Aqsa when the mosque was refurbished, about 1940, and are probably Byzantine in origin.

Other exhibits relating to more recent Islamic history in Jerusalem include the huge cooking pots that were used to prepare food for the city's poor in the 18th century—all 1,120 of them, according to the attached list—and the cannon that throughout the 19th century announced the beginning and end of the fast each day during the month of Ramadan. The museum also features pleasingly uncluttered cases of coins and displays of glass and porcelain.

The tall and spacious halls of this museum make it an inviting place in which to enjoy both architecture and artifacts. The museum also houses an extensive library that includes many documents and plans of Islamic buildings and monuments in Jerusalem; this section is not open to the public.

MUSEUM OF JEWISH ART

Kiryat Banot
55 Harav Zalman Sorotzkin Street
Jerusalem

HOURS: By appointment	TEL.: 02–821298
	ADMISSION: Free

Focus: Sephardi Ritual Objects

As is the case with many institutions in Israel, this museum was created and nourished by one individual. Rabbi Shlomo Pappenheim, its director, began to form the collection of ritual artifacts from the Jewish communities of Morocco, Egypt, Yemen, Syria, Iran, and India in the 1950s, when Jews from North Africa and the Middle East were immigrating to Israel in large numbers.

While the main purpose of the Museum of Jewish Art is to preserve and strengthen the traditions of Sephardi Jewry through an appreciation of its religious art, its collections also include Judaica from Europe representing Ashkenazi traditions, and a group of engaging primitive paintings by Nathan Haber documenting the life and personalities of the Polish *shtetl* in which he lived before coming to Israel.

The museum's collections would benefit from ampler exhibition space, which would enable them to be seen to fuller advantage.

MUSEUM OF NATURAL HISTORY

6 Mohiliver Street
Jerusalem

HOURS: Sun.–Thurs. 9–13 (Mon. and Wed. 16–18 also)	TEL.: 02–631116
	ADMISSION: Free

Focus: Natural History and Elementary Biology

Functioning primarily as an educational resource for Jerusalem school-children, this museum is also frequented by adults and family groups. Its emphasis is on wildlife, biology, and natural history. Exhibits are varied and cover a wide range of natural phenomena. In one area is an active beehive, enclosed in glass, in another a colorful diorama of a Red Sea coral reef. Interacting displays are also featured. The human body and its functions are explained in a section where models of the heart, brain, and digestive system can be activated by push buttons.

Because the Museum of Natural History is most often used by school classes accompanied by their teachers, labels and text panels are minimal. Individual youngsters who visit the museum should therefore be accompanied by an adult able to explain the exhibits.

NAHON MUSEUM OF ITALIAN JUDAICA

27 Hillel Street
Jerusalem

HOURS: Sun. and Tues. 10–13, Wed. 16–19
Other days by appointment

TEL.: 02–241610
ADMISSION: $1.50

Focus: **1701 Synagogue; Ceremonial Art**

Sanctuary of the Conegliano Veneto Synagogue

A position of distinction is generally accorded to Italian Judaica, owing to the excellence of the workmanship and the consistent use of precious metals. This high standard is evident in the ceremonial objects in the collection of the Nahon Museum of Italian Judaica, among which are a silver set for *brit milah* (the circumcision ceremony), covered silver *kiddush* cups, and a *parochet*, or curtain for the Holy Ark, dated 1620 and inscribed "Olivetti–Montefiore," marking it as a gift to the synagogue on the occasion of a marriage between two prominent Italian Jewish families. Its rich red-silk fabric is embroidered with gilded silver thread.

One of the oldest objects in the collection is a ceremonial plaque, or *shiviti*, inscribed with the words "Know before whom you stand." Such plaques—named from the opening word of a verse (Psalms 16:8) in the morning prayer service, "I have set [*shiviti*] the Lord always before me"—are carved in wood, cut out of parchment or paper, or wrought in silver. This example dates from the end of the 15th century, and it is decorated with neoclassical motifs characteristic of the Renaissance period. It was originally hung on the east wall of the Great Synagogue of Padua and miraculously escaped damage in the bombing of the synagogue during World War II.

Also typical of the Italian Jewish tradition is a *maftir* book from the city of Urbino, and a group of amulets for the protection of newborn infants, inscribed with kabbalistic texts.

The centerpiece of the museum is the synagogue of Conegliano Veneto, built in 1701 and transported to Jerusalem in 1952 from its original location in a town some 35 miles from Venice. The synagogue is far from being merely an exhibit; it functions as a place of worship for the Italian Jewish population of Jerusalem, holding Friday evening, Saturday morning, and holiday services.

This small but special museum is centrally located in downtown Jerusalem and is easy to reach.

OLD YISHUV COURT MUSEUM

6 Or Hahayim Street
Jewish Quarter, Old City
Jerusalem

HOURS: Sun.–Thurs. 9–16

TEL.: 02–284636
ADMISSION: $2.00

Focus: **Daily Life in 19th-Century Jerusalem**

The museum derives its name from the term "old *yishuv*" (*yishuv* is the Hebrew word for "settlement"), applied to the small Jewish community that lived in Jerusalem and throughout the country before the arrival of the first Zionist settlers in the 1880s, and from the fact that in the Old City a house was typically built around an interior courtyard shared by several generations or even several families. Also typical of Old City architecture are the building's thick stone walls and domed ceilings, necessitated by the scarcity of wooden roof beams.

The museum occupies the former residence of the Weingarten family, prominent members of the old *yishuv*, who lived here for five generations, until the evacuation of the Jewish Quarter after it fell to the Arabs in 1948. With the reunification of the city in 1967, a younger member of the family, Rivca Weingarten, returned to her former home and began to assemble a

Room of an Ashkenazi family

collection of furniture, clothing, china, and other household goods in an effort to re-create the atmosphere of 19th-century Jewish life in Jerusalem. The museum was subsequently established with the support of the Jerusalem Foundation and private donors and with Rivca Weingarten as its director.

The kitchen is complete with primitive cooking range and such accessories as bowls for kneading dough and a coal-heated iron. Across the hall is a bedroom, with cribs, toys, an old Singer sewing machine, and a special "birth bed," traditionally brought into a household when a baby was expected.

Two rooms in the house demonstrate the diversity of customs within the old *yishuv*, highlighting the characteristic Sephardi and Askhenazi styles. The Sephardi community, whose cultural traditions developed in Spain, North Africa, and the Middle East, commonly used rugs, cushions, and low sofas in their quarters; the Ashkenazim preferred a more Westernized style, importing furniture from Eastern and Central Europe. Clothes also point to differences between the two traditions; the Sephardim, who had lived in Jerusalem longer, adapted to the local garb, while the Ashkenazim continued to dress in the manner of their various European countries of origin.

Exhibited in an adjoining room are tools used by Jerusalem's tradesmen and professionals, among them tinsmiths, carpenters, scribes, and apothecaries. A brass box to hold a bootblack's equipment is particularly handsome. This section of the museum also includes a collection of antique trade signs. Visitors should also note the unusual oval table placed in front of the nearby museum office. It stands on a pedestal supported by four wooden lions holding bunches of grapes in their mouths.

Domestic utensils in the courtyard

Like the interior rooms, the courtyard has features evocative of earlier times: the laundry tubs, the corner where charcoal was stored, and the cistern in which rainwater was collected—the only source of water for the residents. In contrast to the stark stone walls, touches of color appear in the ubiquitous geraniums and in the collection of antique petticoats, chemises, and bloomers hung on a clothesline.

There are two synagogues in the compound. One occupies the room where, according to tradition, Rabbi Yitzhak Ben Shlomo Lurie Ashkenazi, an early proponent of the Jewish mystical tradition of the Kabbalah, was born, in 1534. The other synagogue, Or Hahayim (The Light of Life) was founded by the legendary Rabbi Haim Ben Moses Attar, who arrived in Jerusalem from Morocco in 1742, and it bears the name of one of his works, a biblical commentary.

This museum's depiction of a bygone way of life in Jerusalem offers much of interest to both adults and children.

OPEN EYE SCIENCE CENTER

John Cohen Hall
Givat Ram Campus, Hebrew University
Jerusalem

HOURS: Sun.–Fri. 9–13 (Tues. to 18), Sat. 10–15	TEL.: 02–584285 or 02–584227 ADMISSION: Adults $1.00, children $.75

Focus: Teaching Science through Participation

The Open Eye (Heb. *ayin ro'ah*) Science Center is designed for children aged seven and over. It offers a wide range of interacting exhibits. The aim of Professor Peter Hillman, of the Hebrew University, who created the center, was to interest lay people, and more particularly schoolchildren, in science by making scientific subjects accessible and understandable.

Activities begin in the area outside the center, where young visitors are encouraged to ride the seesaws, which demonstrate principles of basic physics, and look into mirrors that create optical illusions. Inside, the museum features exhibits and participatory experiments dealing with sound, light, magnetism, gravity, and other scientific phenomena. The atmosphere here is relaxed and informal, and members of the staff are always available to explain difficult concepts to interested youngsters.

Children participating in experiments

PALESTINIAN ARAB FOLKLORE CENTER

Ibn Haldoun Street
Jerusalem

HOURS: By appointment

TEL.: 02–283251
ADMISSION: Voluntary contribution

Focus: Palestinian Folkways and Traditional Dress

Established to preserve and make better known the rich folklore and heritage of the Arabs of Palestine, this museum features exhibits illustrating the customs and mores of Palestinian village life, as well as a remarkable collection of traditional costumes. Forming the nucleus of this center of Palestinian research and culture is one of the most important ethnographic collections of its kind.

Social and economic changes brought about by modern technology have greatly decreased the making of traditional fine hand-embroidered garments. All the more precious, therefore, are the dozens of exquisite women's costumes shown on mannequins throughout the museum's galleries. A wedding dress from Beit Dajan, near Jaffa, is made of closely embroidered dark-blue linen; it has a slit skirt and a striped red-silk belt, and the back is decorated with stitching in the wavy pattern characteristic of dresses from the coastal plain. An embroidered headdress adorned with coins is part of this outfit. Other beautiful examples of ceremonial garments come from the Bethlehem region. These are identified by the intricate couching of silk and gold thread on the chest panel and on silk insets in the sides and sleeves. As in most Palestinian embroidery, cross-stitching is extensively used.

The traditions of village life in Galilee are also well represented. From Sasa, near Safed, comes a most unusual woman's green broadcloth coat. A seated female mannequin is dressed in a traditional Galilean mountain outfit consisting of a black raw-silk coat, densely embroidered white cotton trousers, and a silver belt. A stunning example is the costume of a Beduin woman from Khan Yunis, near Gaza. Her dress is embroidered mostly in red. She wears a heavy face covering (Arab. *burgo*) made up of strips of coins, and her headdress is a red and yellow striped silk bonnet decorated with coins and covered by a black cotton veil edged with red appliqué.

Of broader interest, and arranged with equal care, are the scenes portraying traditional village life. Among the activities depicted are the baking of bread in a clay oven, or *tabun*, and the weaving of straw trays from wheat stems (gathered at harvest time, dried, and then dyed in various colors). A silversmith is shown at work making jewelry; nearby sits a village youth wielding bellows to keep the forge fire burning. A woman gracefully balances a jar of water on her head as she stands beside a large trough made of camel skin. And a stonecutter, with his tools at his side, chips away at a rough boulder.

Individual artifacts—head veils, cradles, straw mats, and baskets, and an assortment of men's caps and other headgear—augment the main displays. All the exhibits are well labeled in Arabic and English. The Palestinian Arab Folklore Center is located near the American Colony Hotel.

PALOMBO MUSEUM

Mount Zion
Jerusalem

HOURS: By appointment

TEL: 02-710917
ADMISSION: Free

Focus: **Sculptures of David Palombo**

Now a museum, this large, cavelike space was the studio of the Israeli sculptor David Palombo, who was born in Jerusalem in 1920 and died untimely in a motorcycle accident on Mount Zion in 1967.

Although Palombo is best known for his monumental works, including the gates at Yad Vashem and the Knesset, he also created many smaller sculptures in his own unique style. Some 50 of his works are on display here—in wood, stone, glass, and metal—as well as photographs of some of his other sculptures. When Palombo worked in stone, he created relatively simple, organic forms. In wood he often emphasized the color and texture of the natural grain and hinted at the pattern of growth of the tree or branch. Palombo's most famous welded metal creations are powerful and roughly finished; despite the seemingly disjointed planes and rods they still appear to derive their themes from nature.

The museum, located near Zion Gate, can be identified by its distinctive iron entrance door. Visitors (who have made an appointment) pull the hanging bell cord to gain admittance.

THE ROCKEFELLER MUSEUM
Suleiman Street
Jerusalem

HOURS: Sun.–Thurs. 10–17, Fri. and Sat. 10–14	TEL: 02-282251 ADMISSION: $2.00

Focus: Middle Eastern Archaeology

The Rockefeller Museum, which dominates the plateau opposite the northeastern corner of the Old City wall, contains one of the most important collections of antiquities in the country. The museum's distinctive architecture and its historic location—on the spot from which Godfrey de Bouillon launched his successful attack on the walls of Jerusalem in 1099—make it one of the city's most famous landmarks.

Financed by a $2 million grant in 1927 from John D. Rockefeller II, this superb building was opened in 1938 as the Palestine Archaeological Museum and the headquarters of the British-controlled Palestine Department of Antiquities. It was designed by the well-known British architect Austin S. B. Harrison, whose other projects in Jerusalem include Government House, currently the United Nations Headquarters in the city. Harrison was so bent on the building's exterior being constructed of the whitest stone that a new quarry was opened to supply it, and the stonemasons at once dubbed the stone *mizi harrison* (Harrison's Stone).

Harrison used architectural motifs from many neighboring lands, especially in the museum's rectangular inner courtyard. The tiled pool in the center has a fountain, and the pool's surface is covered with water lilies, rarely seen in Jerusalem. Inscriptions, sarcophagi, and capitals add interest to the shaded arcades around the courtyard.

Inner courtyard

The several exhibition galleries inside the museum are long, narrow halls whose regularly spaced glass cases hold displays that have not been changed since the 1967 War. However, the finds are unique and deserve close study. They include stone tools and skeletal remains of the earliest human inhabitants of Palestine, objects and inscriptions from Mesopotamia and Egypt found in Palestine, and finds from all the major excavations undertaken during the Mandate period, including the biblical cities of Megiddo, Lachish, and Beit She'an. Every period, from the Neolithic to the Byzantine, is well represented, and the totality includes some of the most famous discoveries in the history of Middle Eastern archaeology. Outstanding among these are the clay effigies from Neolithic Jericho, the gold jewelry of Tell el-Ajjul, the large anthropoid clay coffins from Beit She'an, the many historic inscriptions carved in stone, and mosaic floors from numerous ancient synagogues.

In a side gallery, finds from Hisham's Palace, near Jericho, known in Arabic as Khirbet el-Mafjar, are exhibited. Among the decorative elements from this classic Umayyad complex are delightful birds, horses, goats, and human figures—some of them with comical faces—created as decorative elements by Umayyad artisans in the early 8th century. Also noteworthy are fragmentary frescoes and the intricately carved stucco dome of the *diwan*, or entry room to the bathhouse. (The source of these finds, Hisham's Palace, is certainly worth a detour. The palace was destroyed by an earthquake in AD 747, but impressive architectural remains, including pillars, gates, and several extraordinary mosaic floors, can be seen there in situ.)

Portion of mosaic floor from Husifah Synagogue, with inscription Shalom al Yisrael ("Peace on Israel"), 5th–6th century

Stucco ceiling decoration from Hisham's Palace, Jericho, 8th century

Among the many other examples of Islamic art in the Rockefeller Museum are several carved wooden panels from el-Aqsa Mosque, completed by Caliph el-Walid in 714. Severely damaged by the earthquake of 747, the mosque was reconstructed in the 770s and has since then been renovated and repaired many times. Other architectural elements from el-Aqsa can be seen at the Museum for Islamic Art adjacent to the mosque (see page 51).

The Crusader period is represented by an important if limited collection. It includes a fine sculptured head of a German crusader and—most significant—the two carved stone lintels from the portals of the Church of the Holy Sepulchre depicting scenes from the life of Jesus, such as his entry into Jerusalem and the Last Supper. These lintels, already damaged by exposure to the elements, were moved here during the Mandate period to protect them from further deterioration. From a later time is an elaborately crafted model of the church itself, made of wood and inlaid with mother-of-pearl.

In addition to its permanent exhibits, the Rockefeller Museum frequently features temporary exhibits devoted to archaeological themes; they are listed in local newspapers and in the Israel Museum calendar of events. (The Rockefeller Museum is administered by the Israel Museum.) Public lectures on archaeology are presented in the auditorium, generally on Sunday afternoons, throughout the winter months. The museum also has an excellent library and a study collection of pottery and potsherds; both are open to scholars and students by appointment.

SIEBENBERG HOUSE

7 Hagitit Street
Jewish Quarter, Old City
Jerusalem

HOURS: Guided tours are conducted Sun.–Fri. beginning at 12. TEL.: 02–282341
The museum is not open to the public at other times, ADMISSION: $3.00
but group tours can be arranged by appointment.

Focus: Archaeological Remains in the Old City

A personally narrated slide presentation introduces visitors to the private excavations carried out beneath the handsome residence of Belgian-born Theo Siebenberg and his wife, Miriam, an Israeli artist. As the introductory presentation explains, when the Siebenbergs moved here after the 1967 War, excavations in nearby areas of the Jewish Quarter were resulting in important discoveries, and the Siebenbergs decided to explore the basement area below their new house.

More than two decades and several million dollars later, visitors are conducted by Siebenberg along planks to the excavated levels under the house to view the remains of a 2nd-century BC Jewish ritual bath (Heb. *mikveh*), a 5th-century AD Byzantine plastered cistern, and an ancient aqueduct. Displayed in wall niches along the route are some small artifacts: iron nails, a bronze key ring, glass perfume jars, bone spindle whorls, cooking utensils, an inkwell, arrowheads, a 1st-century stone weight, and an unusual 6-inch-long glass rhyton decorated with "antlers," dating from the Second Temple period.

Despite their interesting results and their attractive presentation, the Siebenbergs' excavations have been a source of controversy within the scholarly community because they were conducted without the supervision of trained archaeologists.

*Glass rhyton,
Second Temple
period*

THE SKIRBALL MUSEUM

Hebrew Union College
13 King David Street
Jerusalem

HOURS: Sun.–Thurs. 10–16, Fri. and Sat. 10–14   TEL: 02–232444
ADMISSION: Free

Focus: Archaeology of Tel Dan, Tel Gezer, and Aroer

This museum, a major component of the Skirball Center for Biblical and Archaeological Research, was opened to the public in 1986. Designed by architect Moshe Safdie, it provides exhibition space that is wonderfully airy and light, and the arrangement and presentation of the exhibits reinforce this feeling of spaciousness. Both the floors and the bases of the display cases are of black basalt slabs, reminiscent of the outdoor pavements of the ancient city of Dan in Upper Galilee, where many of the artifacts featured in the museum were discovered. Other building materials, such as limestone and plaster, harmonize with the artifacts on display. Color photomurals, of finds in situ, backed up by models and site plans, offer glimpses into the process of archaeological excavation. Clear maps, drawings, and text panels accompany the exhibits, supplying detailed descriptions, with relevant quotations from the Bible and other sources.

All the finds displayed here come from excavations carried out by the Nelson Glueck School of Biblical Archaeology of the Hebrew Union College in Jerusalem. In addition to Dan, the sites represented include the ancient cities of Gezer, in the foothills between Jaffa and Jerusalem, and Aroer, in the northern Negev. The aim of director Avraham Biran has been to create a museum of sites whose finds illustrate the continuous history of the country from the 2nd millennium BC to the 2nd century AD. Exhibits center on three major themes: fortifications, burial customs, and cultic practices.

Models of excavated city gates provide examples of ancient defensive architecture. These models reproduce a well-preserved gate of the 18th century BC uncovered at Dan (or Laish, as it was called in the Bronze Age); a gate of the 10th century BC from Gezer, built in the Solomonic style; and a gate of the 9th century BC from Dan, constructed when the city belonged to the northern kingdom of Israel. These handsome models of walls and gates are accompanied by plans and photographs of the actual structures as they were uncovered at the various excavations, which make clear the extent of and the evidence for the reconstruction.

In the section on burial customs, finds are displayed against the back-

*Pottery vessels
and model of
fortifications
at Tel Dan*

ground of large photographs of ancient tombs. Noteworthy here is a large clay sarcophagus from Gezer, dating from the 15th–14th century BC, with eight handles attached to its lid.

Among the cultic objects, artifacts from Dan, which was a major religious center in the time of King Jeroboam, at the end of the 10th century BC, are prominent. One exhibit features a large clay bathtub, possibly used for libation or purification. Dating from the 9th and 8th centuries BC are a four-horned altar and an urn filled with ashes and three iron incense shovels that were found beside the altar.

This small museum succeeds in presenting its collection in a way that simplifies archaeology for the layman, yet intrigues the expert. It is within walking distance of most major hotels.

*Clay figurine
of the god Bes
found at Tel Dan*

TICHO HOUSE

7 Harav Kook Street
Jerusalem

HOURS: Sun.–Thurs. 10–17 (Tues. to 22), Fri. 10–14
Café on premises serves light meals, daily 10–24, Fri. 10–15,
Sat. from sundown to midnight.

TEL: 02–245068
ADMISSION: Free

Focus: **Paintings of Anna Ticho**

Ticho House, which was opened to the public in 1984, is located in the center of downtown Jerusalem. Neither a museum nor an art gallery in a strict sense, it offers a chance to relax in quiet surroundings and enjoy a unique mix of Jerusalem's art and history.

The house, built in the early 1860s, was one of the first private villas constructed outside the Old City walls. Originally it was probably owned by a Jerusalem Arab, Aga Rashid, since it bore his name for many years. In the 1880s it was occupied by the family of Moses Shapira, a converted Russian-born Jew and a controversial antiquities dealer. Shapira, his Lutheran German wife, and his daughters spent several years in this house, sharing its spacious garden with doves, dogs, stray cats, a deer, and, at one point, an ostrich; a charming account of the period can be found in *La Petite Fille de Jérusalem*, an autobiographical novel written by one of the daughters, Myriam Harry. The story, however, has an unhappy ending. In 1883, Shapira attempted to sell what he described as an ancient scroll of the Book of Deuteronomy to the British Museum for one million pounds sterling. When the manuscript was declared a forgery, Shapira was discredited and eventually committed suicide.

The house saw a succession of inhabitants before it was changed by Dr. Abraham Ticho into an ophthalmic hospital in 1924. After that, for nearly four decades it served the population of the city, as well as many patients from neighboring Middle Eastern countries, since Dr. Ticho was well known as a specialist in the treatment of trachoma. His wife, artist Anna Ticho (1894–1980), maintained a studio in the family quarters upstairs.

On the ground floor of this typical 19th-century stone building is Dr. Ticho's study, where his library, his collection of Hanukkah lamps, and other items can be seen. On his desk is a letter from Emir Abdullah, grandfather of King Hussein of Jordan, thanking him for the eyeglasses he had prescribed.

On display upstairs are some 70 works by Anna Ticho, who held her first exhibit in this house in 1930. For the most part they are in black and white, since charcoal was the preferred medium for her landscapes of Jerusalem and the surrounding hills and countryside. Only in her late seventies did Ticho begin to use some color in her realistic yet nonfigurative works, which grew larger and bolder with time. She continued to work in her studio here until her death in 1980 at the age of eighty-six. In her will, Ticho bequeathed this house to the people of Jerusalem. It is administered by the Israel Museum.

Hill of Jerusalem *by Anna Ticho*

THE TOURJEMAN POST

1 Hail Hahandasah Street
Corner Derech Shechem (Damascus Road)
Jerusalem

HOURS: Sun.–Thurs. 9–16 (Tues. to 18), Fri. 9–13   TEL.: 02–281278
ADMISSION: $1.00

Focus: **The Battles for Jerusalem in the 20th Century**

Built by Hassan Bey Tourjeman of rose-colored Jerusalem stone (Arab. *mizzi ahmar*), the house is typical of affluent Arab residences in Jerusalem in the 1930s. Located at the edge of the Israeli section of the city, the building was badly damaged during the war in 1948; later it served as an Israeli military post, standing like a sentinel over the nearby Mandelbaum Gate, which was for almost two decades the only border crossing between Israel and Jordan. In 1967, when the city was reunited and the barbed wire dismantled, the Tourjeman house was partially restored by the Jerusalem Foundation. But some fortifications were left in place, and the scars of battle were not patched over, since the house was converted into a museum devoted to demonstrating the destructiveness of war and the tragedy of a city divided for nineteen years.

It is best to start the tour of the Tourjeman Post from the rooftop, where a sweeping panorama of Jerusalem serves as an introduction to the historical exhibits inside. Clear labels identify all the major points of interest: Mount Scopus, the Mount of Olives, the Old City, 19th-century Jewish neighborhoods, easily identified by their red-tiled roofs, and the minarets and church steeples of the city's Muslim and Christian neighborhoods.

Inside are photographs, relief maps, and documents illustrating Jerusalem's recent past. An excellent pamphlet (in Hebrew, English, and Arabic) available here provides background information about a period—beginning with the British occupation in 1917—often neglected when the history of this ancient city is told.

WOHL ARCHAEOLOGICAL MUSEUM/THE HERODIAN QUARTER

Hurvah Square, Corner Ha-Karaim Road
Jewish Quarter, Old City
Jerusalem

HOURS: Sun.–Thurs. 9–17, Fri. 9–13

TEL.: 02–282005
ADMISSION: $2.00
(includes admission to the Burnt House)

Focus: **Mansions of the Herodian Period**

The Wohl Archaeological Museum, which opened in 1987, contains the remains of six mansions from the time of the Herodian dynasty (37 BC–AD 70) and artifacts uncovered in those houses. The Herodian mansions, like the Burnt House (see page 14), are among the important discoveries made in the Jewish Quarter between 1969 and 1983 by the archaeological team led by Professor Nahman Avigad. Built in what was known as the Upper City, on the slope of the western hill facing the Temple Mount, the mansions belonged to Jerusalem's nobility, headed by the high priest.

The museum is located underground, below the religious school Yeshivat Hakotel. Descending 10 feet from street level, visitors find themselves 2,000 years back in time, walking on the actual floors of the opulent mansions. Isometric views, site plans, text panels, and a scale model of one of the man-

Room in the "Palatial Mansion" with stone table and storage jars and mosaic floor

sions re-create life among Jerusalem's elite during the last century of the Second Temple period, before the city and the Temple were destroyed by the Romans, in AD 70.

Clearly visible are the basements and ground-level remains of the mansions, which were originally two or even three stories high. Each mansion, built around a central courtyard paved with flagstones, contained at least one ritual bath, or *mikveh*, in addition to other baths, storage rooms with vaulted ceilings, and plastered cisterns. Also preserved are several fine mosaic floors with geometric designs in black, red, and white. (Depictions of persons or animals were rare in Herodian Jerusalem owing to the proscription in Jewish law of graven images.)

The largest house excavated, covering an area of 2,000 square feet and containing five ritual baths, was dubbed by the archaeologists "The Palatial

Mansion"; it may have been the residence of the high priest. In one of its spacious reception rooms are several rare stone tables and large stone storage jars found during the excavations. The walls bear evidence of ancient remodeling: originally decorated with colorful frescoes, they were later replastered in white stucco, with patterns resembling paneled masonry.

"The Peristyle House," so named for the colonnade that surrounds its open court, is similar in design to villas in Pompeii. Carved pillars and a grouping of architectural elements—capitals, sections of friezes with floral or egg-and-dart motifs, molded stucco fragments—hint at the former grandeur of the structure, as does a reconstruction of a floor in a geometrical design in gray and pink stones in the technique called *opus sectile*. This type of mosaic, popular in Rome, has been found in Israel only at two of Herod's palaces, in Jericho and in Masada.

The southernmost house in this residential section has not been restored. Next to it is an untouched heap of stones and ashes, evidence of the destruction and fire brought on by the Romans in AD 70.

Artifacts excavated in or near the mansions are chronologically arranged in display cases throughout the museum. The earliest finds are from the 8th and 7th centuries BC, proving that the city had already spread to this hill, west of the Temple Mount, during the First Temple period. (The size and shape of Jerusalem during that period have been the topic of much scholarly debate.) Among the finds are many clay objects: jars, plates, bowls, oil lamps, stamped jar handles. Terra-cotta fertility figurines indicate that not everyone in Jerusalem observed the ban on graven images. Artifacts from the Hasmonean period include housewares such as storage jars, cooking pots, bowls, and oil lamps.

By far the most luxurious items displayed here, many imported from other countries, are from the Herodian period. They include delicate pottery decorated with floral designs, glass vessels, wine amphorae from Italy, terra sigillata ware, objects made of bone (such as cosmetic spoons, dice, and spindle whorls), and two portable sundials made of soft limestone. Stone vessels, used extensively by the wealthy inhabitants of the Herodian mansions—from large jars and trays to cups and goblets—are of special interest; according to Jewish law, stone vessels, like glass ones, are not susceptible to ritual uncleanness. A rare glass pitcher, now on display at the Israel Museum, was excavated here (the spot where it was found is marked by an actual-size drawing of it). Only slightly damaged by the fire that consumed the city, the pitcher bears the inscription, in Greek, "Ennion made it." Ennion was a noted glassmaker of the 1st century AD who lived in Sidon.

A sweeping panorama of the Temple Mount greets visitors as they leave the museum, a view similar to the one enjoyed by the residents of the Herodian mansions some 2,000 years ago.

WOLFSON MUSEUM

**Hechal Shlomo
58 King George Street
Jerusalem**

HOURS: Sun.–Thurs. 9–13, Fri. 9–12

TEL.: 02–247112
ADMISSION: $1.00

Focus: Jewish Ceremonial Art

*Silver
amulets
from
Afghanistan,
Persia, and
Morocco,
18th–19th
century*

The Sir Isaac and Lady Edith Wolfson Museum, located in the Hechal
Shlomo building complex, seat of the Ashkenazi Chief Rabbinate of Israel,
contains an excellent collection of Jewish ceremonial art reflecting the traditions of Jews in many different cultures—communities in Eastern and Western Europe, as well as in India, Afghanistan, Yemen, and North Africa.

The collections include examples of most of the major art forms employed to enhance the observance of Judaism. Some of these objects celebrate the events of the life cycle. Here are intricately decorated and inscribed amulets in silver and parchment, some intended to protect mother and newborn child, others to ward off the evil eye; the *mohel*'s circumcision knives and record books; trays used for the *pidion haben*, the ceremony of the redemption of the firstborn son; and ornate *ketubbot*, or marriage contracts, from various parts of the Diaspora. Other objects highlight the cycle of the Jewish year, and the museum makes a point of arranging exhibits appropriate to every major festival. Featured at the time of Purim, for example, are plates on which

Parochet
*(Torah curtain)
from Germany,
1716*

friends and neighbors send one another gifts of food, wooden molds for baking Purim cakes, and a varied collection of scrolls and cases of the Book of Esther.

To commemorate the museum's acquisition of the important Howitt and Goldnitzki collections of Judaica, the Wolfson Museum published a book that provides illustrations and explanations of many of the most important items.

YAD VASHEM

Holocaust Martyrs and Survivors Remembrance
Mount of Remembrance
Jerusalem

HOURS: Sun.–Thurs. 9–17, Fri. 9–14
Cafeteria on premises

TEL.: 02–531202
ADMISSION: Free

Focus: **History of the Holocaust**

Hall of Remembrance, Yad Vashem

Visiting Yad Vashem is a solemn pilgrimage that everyone must make, not only to be reminded of the enormous tragedy of the Holocaust but also to come to a full understanding of the role and the reality of modern Israel. Yad Vashem—the words mean "a monument and a name" (Isaiah 56:5)—is a place of records. It looks into the darkest side of human nature, yet it also records deeds of self-sacrifice, courage, and love. Above all, its avowed goal is to preserve the memory of the victims of the Holocaust so that a similar catastrophe may never happen again.

The Yad Vashem complex is situated on a mountain slope overlooking the village of Ein Karem. The awe-inspiring Hall of Remembrance honors the victims of the Holocaust. The Central Archives of the Holocaust and Heroism house over 50,000,000 documents. In the Avenue for the Righteous Among the Nations, over 500 trees are planted to honor heroic Gentiles who risked their lives to save Jews during the Holocaust. In the Hall of Names are the "Pages of Testimony," recording over three million victims, and commemorative books on the destroyed Jewish communities of Europe.

Open areas contain a number of striking memorial sculptures. These works of art speak of death, sorrow, remembrance, and hope. *Auschwitz* by Elsa Pollak, a survivor of the camp, is in the form of a pillar, suggesting a chimney, inscribed with the serial numbers of Auschwitz inmates. *The Pillar of Heroism* by Israeli sculptor Buki Schwartz, severe in gray stainless steel, commemorates the Jewish resistance. The *Memorial to the Victims of the Death Camps* by Nandor Gild has attenuated bodies and limbs reaching toward the skies. At the end of a menorah-shaped sunken plaza is Bernie Fink's *Soldiers', Ghetto-Fighters', and Partisans' Monument*; the inner edges of its six oblong granite blocks, symbolizing the six million Jews who perished in the Holocaust, form a Star of David, and the star is pierced by a giant steel sword. There are many other sculptures throughout Yad Vashem; the artists include Zvi Aldubi, Naftali Bezem, Ilana Gur, Eli Ilan, Mordechai Kafri, Lea Michelson, and Nathan Rapoport. Boris Saktsier's *Janusz Korczak with Children* enshrines the memory of the Polish physician and educator who accompanied his charges—200 orphans—into the Treblinka-bound cattle cars.

Next to the memorial site, in the open, is the Valley of the Destroyed Communities, where the names of 5,000 of those lost communities, in 22 countries, are engraved on dramatic rocky structures cut into the hill. The Children's Memorial, dedicated to the million and a half children killed by the Nazis, was designed by Moshe Safdie; the one flickering candle in the center of this large underground hall is reflected hundreds of thousands of times through mirrors.

The gates of the Hall of Remembrance were created by artists David Palombo and Bezalel Schatz. The interior walls are made of dressed basalt boulders, and into the gray mosaic floor are worked the names of the 22 largest death camps. An eternal light shines in front of a small vault containing ashes gathered from the camps. Daylight comes in through the space between the wall and the roof, which is built in the form of a huge concrete marquee. The overwhelming silence is sometimes broken by the sounds of birds flying in

Janusz Korczak with Children *by Boris Saktsier, Yad Vashem*

through this space and soon escaping to the daylight again.

The Art Museum mounts exhibitions of works by survivors of the Holocaust and selections from the thousands of drawings and paintings found in the camps, many of them hidden away by their soon-to-perish creators.

The Memorial to the Victims of the Death Camps
by Nandor Gild, Yad Vashem

At the heart of the Yad Vashem complex is the Historical Museum of the Holocaust and Heroism, in which the entire story of the destruction of European Jewry is told chronologically and methodically through original documents, photographs, and artifacts. Exhibits illustrate and detail the richness and diversity of Jewish life in Europe before the war, the rise of Hitler, Germany's expansionist conquests, and, finally, the persecution and destruction of the Jews: the trains, the forced labor, the gas chambers, the crematoria—evidences of vicious inhumanity that it is impossible for the mind to accept.

Near the exit is a single shoe, a torn leather shoe, a child's shoe. It brings the vast tragedy down to human scale. This is everyone's child.

Scene in a death camp, Yad Vashem

THE BIBLE LANDS MUSEUM JERUSALEM

Corner of Granot and Burla Streets
Jerusalem

Projected opening date: 1989

Focus: **Archaeology of Ancient Israel, Egypt, and Mesopotamia**

On permanent exhibition in this museum, which has been under construction since 1987, will be approximately 2,500 artifacts illustrating the material cultures of the ancient societies that laid the foundation of the Judeo-Christian civilization: Sumer, Assyria, Babylon, ancient Israel, Egypt, Persia, Greece, Rome, and Byzantium. The organization of the exhibits in this modern structure, designed by architect Zeev Schoenberg, will follow the chronology of the Bible.

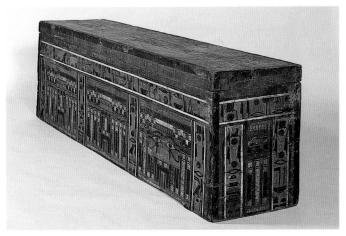

Painted wooden (cedar) coffin from Egypt, c. 2000 BC

The main purpose of the museum is to promote a deeper understanding of the Bible. Dr. Elie Borowski, the collector who, over many years, amassed the ancient artifacts to be housed here, is a survivor of the Holocaust and believes that a return to moral values based on an understanding of the Bible may prevent the occurrence of such tragedies in the future.

The program of the museum will include the occasional showing of temporary exhibitions, focused on specific themes, to enhance the impact of the permanent collection.

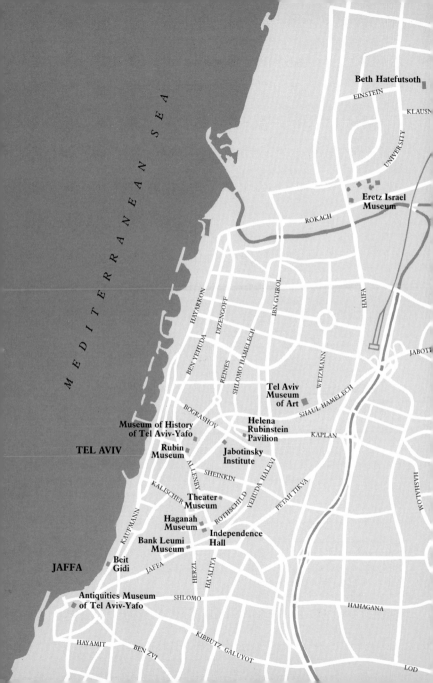

Beth Hatefutsoth

EINSTEIN

KLAUSN

UNIVERSITY

Eretz Israel
Museum

ROKACH

HAIFA

JABOTI

HAYARKON

DIZENGOFF

IBN GVIROL

BEN YEHUDA

REINES

SHLOMO HAMELECH

WEIZMANN

SHAUL HAMELECH

Tel Aviv
Museum
of Art

BOGRASHOV

Helena
Rubinstein
Pavilion

KAPLAN

Museum of History
of Tel Aviv-Yafo

TEL AVIV

Rubin
Museum

Jabotinsky
Institute

ALLENBY

SHEINKIN

YEHUDA HALEVI

PETAH TIKVA

HASHALOM

KALISCHER

Theater
Museum

ROTHSCHILD

KAUFMANN

Haganah
Museum

Bank Leumi
Museum

Independence
Hall

JAFFA

Beit
Gidi

JAFFA

HERZL

HAALIYA

Antiquities Museum
of Tel Aviv-Yafo

SHLOMO

HAHAGANA

HAYAMIT

BEN ZVI

KIBBUTZ GALUYOT

LOD

MEDITERRANEAN SEA

TEL AVIV

ANTIQUITIES MUSEUM OF TEL AVIV–YAFO

10 Mifratz Shlomo Street
Jaffa

HOURS: Sun., Mon., Wed., Thurs., Fri. 9–13, Tues. 16–19, Sat. 10–14

TEL.: 03–825375
ADMISSION: $1.50

Focus: Archaeology of the Port City of Jaffa

Opposite: Gatepost from Jaffa with titles of Ramses II, 13th century BC

Jewish tombstone inscribed in Hebrew and Greek

An overview of the history of the ancient port city of Jaffa (Yafo in Hebrew) is provided by the collections in this museum, a former Turkish *hammam*, or bathhouse. On display in its spacious halls are artifacts found in Jaffa and its vicinity—a fertile region inhabited since prehistoric times. The earliest remains are from the Chalcolithic period; of exceptional interest is a reconstruction of a human burial of that period. Other exhibits include Canaanite pottery and figurines of the goddess Astarte, an Early Iron Age incised basalt bowl, and many examples of Byzantine glass. Exhibits are clearly labeled in both Hebrew and English. The museum is administered by the Eretz Israel Museum.

Jaffa is perhaps most widely remembered because of its role in the Bible as the royal port of King Solomon (II Chronicles 2:15) and as the harbor from which Jonah set out on his ill-fated voyage (Jonah 1:3). References to the city are also found in ancient Egyptian and Mesopotamian chronicles. The museum has a copy of one of the most important of these—a clay prism of King Sennacherib; its cuneiform inscription details an Assyrian campaign against Jaffa and other coastal cities in 701 BC.

The archaeological collection here is but one of the many appealing features of Old Jaffa. Nearby are the numerous shops, art galleries, artists' studios, and open-air restaurants that have made Jaffa's reconstructed harbor area one of the country's most popular attractions.

BANK LEUMI MUSEUM

35 Yehuda Halevi Street
Tel Aviv

HOURS: Sun.–Fri. 9–13   TEL: 03–648981
ADMISSION: Free

Focus: Story of Bank Leumi

The Bank Leumi Museum tells the story of modern banking activity in the country and its connection with the history of Jewish settlement. Located on the street level of the main bank building in downtown Tel Aviv, the museum exhibits a variety of documents, models of several bank buildings, early printing machines, and a collection of 19th- and early-20th-century bank notes and coins.

A short videotape presents the history of Bank Leumi from its origin as a special treasury for Jewish settlement in Palestine, first conceived by Theodor Herzl, the founder of modern Zionism. Officially chartered as the Anglo-Palestine Company in 1899, it was renamed the Anglo-Palestine Bank during the Mandate period. With the establishment of the State of Israel, in 1948, it became Bank Leumi, the "National Bank." From the very beginning, its purpose was to advance the development of agriculture, commerce, and industry in the country.

Among the most interesting items exhibited are an extract from a register of 1900 showing a share held by Dr. Theodor Herzl, an antique typewriter used by the officers of the Jewish Colonial Trust, and the 1948 charter granted to the bank by the Provisional Government of the new Jewish state. There is also a model of the first branch of the Anglo-Palestine Bank, a modest building on Bustrus Street in Jaffa—a far cry from today's Bank Leumi, with its 400 branches all over the world.

BEIT GIDI

Herbert Samuel Boulevard
Tel Aviv

HOURS: Sun.–Thurs. 9–14, Fri. 9–12

TEL.: 03–652044
ADMISSION: $1.00

Focus: **Battle for Jaffa in 1948**

Located on the seashore, near the pre-1948 border between Arab Jaffa and Jewish Tel Aviv, Beit Gidi houses the records of the events that led to the Jewish conquest of Jaffa in the 1948 War. This area of the city, heavily damaged in that war, has since been cleared for urban renewal. Even though partially demolished, this building was spared and has been imaginatively restored. Its lower half is the original stone structure; the upper portion is dark tinted glass.

To the left of the door of the museum is a plaque with the emblem of Irgun Tzvai Leumi, or National Military Organization, the underground group (known also by the acronym Etzel) led by Menachem Begin in its struggle against the British. The emblem, consisting of a raised hand clutching a rifle, superimposed on a map of Palestine and Transjordan, includes as its slogan the Hebrew phrase *rak kach* ("Only thus").

The permanent exhibit at Beit Gidi describes the day-by-day events of the battle for Jaffa, from November 29, 1947, to May 5, 1948. Newspaper clippings, notes, letters, documents, and photographs, together with antique guns and makeshift weapons, re-create the tense atmosphere of the period and illumine developments in the political and military arenas. While there are only a few text panels, and most documents are neither enlarged nor translated into English, the museum's photographs are very good. One shows a young, bearded Menachem Begin disguised as a rabbi, as he appeared during his years as a fugitive from the British authorities.

A special room at Beit Gidi serves as a memorial to those who fell in the battle for Jaffa, among them the fighter who went by the name of Gidi. The museum is dedicated to "the liberators of Jaffa."

BETH HATEFUTSOTH

The Nahum Goldmann Museum of the Jewish Diaspora
Klausner Street, Ramat Aviv
Tel Aviv

HOURS: Sun.–Thurs. 10–17 (Wed. to 19)	TEL.: 03–425161
Cafeteria on premises	ADMISSION: $3.00

Focus: Jewish Life in the Diaspora

Beth Hatefutsoth, the Museum of the Jewish Diaspora, relates the story of a people that was scattered all over the world and yet has remained one family. Its approach to the history of 2,500 years of the Diaspora is original and unconventional. While most museums collect, preserve, and display authentic objects of historical or artistic importance, there are no such artifacts here. In re-creating the communities of the Diaspora, so many of which have been totally destroyed, Beth Hatefutsoth features specially designed and built visual aids that bring history to life.

The concepts through which the Diaspora story is told are thematic rather than chronological; they include Family, Community, Faith, Culture, Life Among the Nations, and Return. In the Community section, dioramas bring viewers into typical yeshiva, synagogue, hospital, law court, and burial society scenes. The theme of Faith is illustrated by scale models of synagogues

Replica of the Arch of Titus

from a wide variety of lands and historical periods. Among the noteworthy models are those of the 2nd-century BC synagogue in Sardis, Turkey, and the synagogue of Worms, Germany, built in 1034, destroyed in 1938, and rebuilt after World War II. Other synagogues featured are those of Kaifeng, China, built in 1163; Toledo, Spain, built in 1200; Cochin, India, built in 1568. Vilna, Amsterdam, and Fez, in Morocco, are also represented. These superb models show architectural details, characteristic regional building materials, and interior furnishings reflecting the diverse cultural environments.

Each of the other themes is developed through appropriate visual means. The museum's presentations utilize the most modern visual aids. These include mini-cinemas that present documentary films to groups, and study

Scale model of Rashi's study in Worms

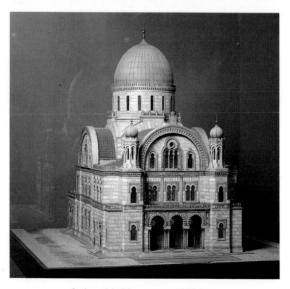

Scale model of the synagogue of Florence

Painted ceiling of scale model of wooden synagogue of Chodorov (Poland)

areas with video booths where individual visitors can watch documentaries of their choice. There are also slide presentations, some of which simultaneously employ 32 projectors on 16 screens. Computer terminals provide visitors with immediate access to over 3,000 articles in Hebrew and English, historical information about almost any Jewish community in the world, as well as genealogical data. A chronological summation of the museum's exhibits is presented in the Chronosphere, a dome-shaped auditorium.

Beth Hatefutsoth, the Museum of the Jewish Diaspora, can lay claim to offering a unique experience. It is an experience that should be allotted ample time.

ERETZ ISRAEL MUSEUM

2 University Street
Ramat Aviv
Tel Aviv

HOURS: Sun.–Fri. 9–13 (Tues. 16–19 also),
Sat. 10–13
Refreshments available at cafeteria and kiosk

TEL.: 03–415244
ADMISSION: $4.00

Focus: **The Land of Israel: Archaeology, Ethnography, History**

Coins from Syracuse (Sicily), 5th century BC

The Eretz Israel Museum, formerly known as the Ha'aretz Museum, was established in 1953. Its pavilions are scattered over 30 acres on the northern bank of the Yarkon River on the northern edge of Tel Aviv. As its name indicates (*Eretz Israel* means "the land of Israel"), the museum specializes in topics relating to the history, culture, and people of the country.

The museum is constantly growing and changing. Instead of compartmentalizing the collections according to artifact type or historical period, director Rehavam Ze'evi has encouraged the presentation of integrated, lifelike reproductions of authentic experiences in ancient Israel through the use of both original artifacts and replicas, as well as through sophisticated audiovisual techniques. Thus the Nehuhstan Pavilion, devoted to the history of mining and metallurgy in the lands of the Bible, utilizes models and reconstructions to illustrate copper extraction in early times. They include a model of an ancient mine, as well as finds from archaeological excavations.

The nearby Ceramics Pavilion features the uses of clay as a raw material and the methods of pottery making in various ancient cultures. A reconstruction of an ancient Israelite house illustrates the place of clay vessels within the home and their many uses in daily life.

The Kadman Numismatic Pavilion traces the development of monetary systems and the use of coinage through selected examples from its collection of approximately 80,000 ancient coins. Other materials are displayed here, such as busts of emperors and rulers whose images appear on many of the coins. Together with enlarged photographs, the extensive text panels demonstrate the historic and archaeological importance of the individual coins.

The Ethnography and Folklore Pavilion displays religious artifacts used on holidays, as well as scenes of daily life in various communities. The diversity of costumes and jewelry shown here is most interesting; noteworthy is a Yemenite wedding scene. Another high point is the reconstructed synagogue of Trino Vercelles, brought here from the Italian Piedmont. Its original 17th-century furniture includes a highly ornate Holy Ark.

The theme of the Man and His Work Pavilion is the development of ancient production methods. It was created by Professor Shmuel Avitsur to demonstrate to 20th-century audiences the traditional techniques of fishing, hunting, husbandry, transportation, and construction—techniques that changed little between the time of the Bible and the late 1800s. A focal point in the pavilion is a reconstructed Middle Eastern *suq*, or marketplace, where

Weaving demonstration

Ancient glass vessels

Glassblowing demonstration

artisans are at work: a woman weaver at a 19th-century handloom, a tinsmith mending a leaky bucket, a potter throwing a lump of clay on a wheel.

Some of the most intriguing exhibits here are connected with the Bread Cycle—the production, from planting to harvesting, of one of mankind's basic foods. On view are wooden plows, grain pits, storage bins, millstones, and even a reconstruction of a threshing floor, where a donkey separates the wheat from the chaff. At the end of the cycle, a baker mixes flour and water, kneads the dough and flattens it, and then lays it on the surface of a metal dome heated by charcoal. The smell of fresh bread permeates the *suq*, and visitors are often invited to enjoy the steaming pita. The large Roman wine press near the exit was discovered during construction work for the exhibition halls.

Philistine remains at Tell Qasile excavation

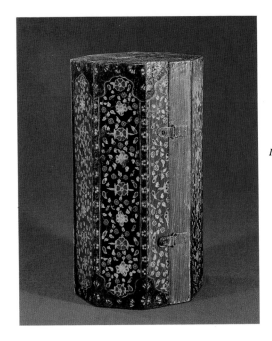

Painted wooden Torah case from Yemen, 19th century

More traditional display techniques predominate in the Glass Pavilion, which features an exceptionally fine collection. Many of the objects displayed here were bequeathed to the museum by its founder, Dr. Walter Moses. Exhibits proceed chronologically, from the earliest, core-wound Egyptian glass vessels of the 14th century BC through the mold-made and blown glass vessels of the Roman and Byzantine periods. Among the noteworthy products of the Roman period is a rare blue vase signed by the famous 1st-century glassmaker Ennion. A late 14th-century mosque lamp decorated in gold and enamel shows the continuance of glassmaking under Islam.

Among the other attractions of the Eretz Israel Museum are the Lasky Planetarium and a park featuring typical landscapes of the Holy Land, with terraces, watchtowers, and a vineyard. A traditional oil press and a small plaza with sundials from all over the country should also be noted.

A most unusual feature of this museum is the archaeological excavations being conducted within its enclosure, which occupies the site of Tell Qasile, a town founded by the Philistines about 1200 BC. A team headed by Dr. Amihai Mazar of the Hebrew University has uncovered 12 superimposed settlement levels so far. Visitors can view the remains of some unique Philistine temples and enter the reconstructed private houses and courtyards of the late Iron Age. A few of the artifacts excavated here are on display in a building nearby; the beautiful shapes and decorations of the clay vessels belie the reputation of the Philistines as barbarians.

The Eretz Israel Museum is one of Tel Aviv's most important cultural centers and provides activities and exhibits of great interest to both children and adults. Visitors should allow plenty of time for a visit to this multifaceted museum.

HAGANAH MUSEUM/BEIT ELIAHU

23 Rothschild Boulevard
Tel Aviv

HOURS: Sun.–Thurs. 9–15, Fri. 9–12:30

TEL.: 03–623624
ADMISSION: $1.00

Focus: **Founding and History of the Haganah**

Two adjacent buildings—a modern three-story structure and a small house dating from the early days of Tel Aviv—make up this museum. In the small house, Eliahu Golomb, who, with Dov Hoz, founded the Haganah in 1920, lived until his death in 1945.

After viewing the rooms where Golomb lived and worked, with their typical 1930s furnishings, visitors can proceed to the adjoining building and view exhibits devoted to the history of the Haganah, the Jewish underground organization, whose name is the Hebrew word for "defense." Haganah activities during the Arab disturbances in the 1930s and during the struggle against the British after World War II are chronicled here. Models of the "tower and stockade" settlements—built in many cases in a single night by Jewish pioneers in the 1930s—are shown. The exhibits in the modern part of this museum also cover the founding of the Israeli army. Some of the major battles crucial to the survival of Israel are re-created, and one section deals with the theme of heroism in battle.

The museum features a large collection of uniforms and paramilitary outfits worn by Jewish, Arab, and British forces in Palestine over a period of 30 years, as well as a display of the weapons they used. The Haganah Museum is a valuable source for those interested in military history. Many of the documents and some of the labels are in Hebrew only.

INDEPENDENCE HALL

16 Rothschild Boulevard
Tel Aviv

HOURS: Sun.–Fri. 9–13, Sat. 10–14

TEL.: 03–653942
ADMISSION: $1.50

Focus: First Days of the State of Israel

Site of the signing of the Declaration of Independence of the State of Israel

It was here in Independence Hall that David Ben-Gurion announced the establishment of the State of Israel. This building, selected for the historic ceremony because its bunker-like ground floor offered a measure of security, was originally the home of Meir Dizengoff, first mayor of Tel Aviv. Mayor Dizengoff gave it to the city for the establishment of an art museum, and the Tel Aviv Museum of Art (see page 103) was located here from 1932 until 1959, when it moved to larger quarters. In the mid-1980s the decision was made to restore the main hall to its appearance on the day when independence was declared and to make it a museum.

In the entrance hall, an exhibit features the history of two motifs: the menorah, which appears on the official seal of the State of Israel, and the Star of David, which appears on Israel's flag. Elsewhere in the museum, exhibits chronicle the period from November 29, 1947, when the United Nations voted to partition Palestine, to May 14, 1948, when the State of Israel was officially established. Emphasized are the events of Israel's struggle for survival in the first months of its existence.

Independence Hall is administered by the Eretz Israel Museum.

JABOTINSKY INSTITUTE

Jabotinsky Building
38 King George Street
Tel Aviv

HOURS: Sun.–Thurs. 8–15, Fri. 8–13	TEL.: 03–290211 or 03–287320
Cafeteria in building	ADMISSION: $.50

Focus: **Life and Ideology of Ze'ev (Vladimir) Jabotinsky**

Located on the second floor of the Jabotinsky Building in Tel Aviv are a small museum, a library, and archives that make up the Jabotinsky Institute, which deals with the life of Ze'ev (Vladimir) Jabotinsky (1880–1940) and with the history of the various Jewish resistance movements that he inspired.

Born in Russia, Jabotinsky at the age of twenty-three fell under the spell of Theodor Herzl. Later, however, Jabotinsky condemned the Zionist movement's timidity in its relations with the authorities of the British Mandate and its passivity in the face of growing opposition by the Arabs of Palestine. In 1925 he broke away from the Zionist Organization and founded the Zionist Revisionist movement, which advocated the establishment—after a Jewish majority had been achieved through mass immigration—of a "self-governing Jewish commonwealth" in Palestine and Transjordan. Jabotinsky gained considerable support among those who felt that Zionism was not solving the problems of anti-Semitism and that the British, under Arab pressure, were retreating from their promise of a National Home for the Jews in Palestine. Although Jabotinsky did not live to see the establishment of the State of Israel, his political heirs—the leaders of the Likud party—continue to play a decisive role.

Photographs, letters, newspapers, and memorabilia illustrate the events of Jabotinsky's life and the policies he espoused. The letters—written in Hebrew, Yiddish, French, Russian, and Spanish—indicate the range of Jabotinsky's correspondence with Zionist and world political figures. A wide selection of the books and articles he wrote is also on display. Exhibits trace the beginning of Jewish organized defense against the Arabs following the riots of 1920 and Jabotinsky's arrest by the British.

Other exhibits deal with the Jewish Battalions in World War I, illegal Jewish immigration into Palestine during the Mandate period, and the establishment of Betar, the Revisionist youth movement. Betar gained popularity among the Jewish youth of prewar Poland; photographs show some of its members in their paramilitary uniforms—brown shirts and caps. Also documented are Jabotinsky's strenuous objections to the 1937 Peel Commission plan for the partition of Palestine.

Newspaper clippings and letters record the reaction to Jabotinsky's sudden death in 1940 in New York City. In his will he wrote: "My remains will be transferred [to Eretz Israel] only on the instructions of a Jewish government." In 1965, twenty-five years after his death and seventeen years after the founding of the State of Israel, his remains were brought to Jerusalem and buried on Mount Herzl in a state funeral.

A special display retells the episode of the sinking of the *Altalena* in 1948, which still provokes bitter debate in Israel. This ship, purchased by the Revisionist Irgun Tzvai Leumi—the National Military Organization, also known by the acronym Etzel—to bring arms and ammunition to its members, became the focus of an intense and violent conflict shortly after the establishment of the State of Israel. Etzel leaders on board refused to accede to Ben-Gurion's demand that all arms be handed over to the Israel Defense Forces, the army of the new state, and shots were exchanged between ship and shore. The *Altalena* eventually exploded and sank, with the loss of over 80 lives.

While most of the individual labels in this museum are in both English and Hebrew, many of the text panels in Hebrew are not translated. However, brochures with English translations are available on request at the office, and inquiries are welcomed by the museum staff.

MUSEUM OF THE HISTORY OF TEL AVIV–YAFO

27 Bialik Street
Tel Aviv

HOURS: Sun., Mon., Wed., Thurs., Fri. 9–13, Tues. 16–19	TEL.: 03–653534 or 03–653052 ADMISSION: $2.00

Focus: **Development of Tel Aviv**

Housed, appropriately enough, in the former City Hall of Tel Aviv is the Museum of the History of Tel Aviv–Yafo. (*Yafo* is the Hebrew form of Jaffa.) A handsome building with a convex facade, it was designed by architect M. Czerner and was built in 1925; it was renovated and reopened as a museum in 1971. It is administered by the Eretz Israel Museum.

Documents, maps, photographs, models, and dioramas effectively illustrate the growth of the first all-Jewish city of modern times from its establish-

Queen Esther's Crown

ment on the sand dunes north of the ancient port city of Jaffa in 1909. The space within the museum is utilized to the full: under the staircase, for example, is a whimsical array of old street signs, street lamps, and outdated traffic lights.

By "walking" through re-creations of several late-19th-century overcrowded neighborhoods of Jaffa, visitors can gain an understanding of the reasons for the establishment of the new city to the north. They can also "watch" the drawing of lots for building sites in the sand dunes, an area that was envisioned as "the garden city" of Tel Aviv. Photographs show the city's first water tower, which also housed the municipal offices, fire brigade, first-aid station, and post office. The development of the city's water supply, lighting, and systems of public transportation from horse-drawn coach to airplane are documented. Other exhibits trace the gradual merging of autonomous neighborhoods into a unified city, with Tel Aviv's incorporation as a municipality in 1934.

There are also photomurals of the conflicts and battles that have been part of Tel Aviv's history, beginning with World War I, when the Ottoman authorities ordered the forced evacuation of its citizens, and including the Arab riots of the 1920s and 1930s. A special area of the museum is a memorial to the Israeli pilots who perished in the defense of Tel Aviv in 1948. Visitors can also view a multiscreen slide presentation entitled "24 Hours in the Life of the City," with titles in Hebrew and English.

A highlight is the office of the first mayor of the city, Meir Dizengoff, restored to appear as it was during his days in office. Among the memorabilia here is one of Dizengoff's personal trademarks: the straw hat he wore as, riding his white horse, he made his daily inspection tours of the city.

The museum has a library that is open to the public. Its collection of books, archival material, documents, and photographs are a valuable source of information about the history of Tel Aviv. Not all the text panels have been translated into English, but an information sheet in English is available on request at the entrance.

RUBIN MUSEUM
14 Bialik Street
Tel Aviv

HOURS: Sun., Mon., Wed., Thurs. 10–14, Tues. 10–13 and 16–20, Sat. 11–14	TEL.: 03–658961 ADMISSION: $1.50

Focus: Life and Work of Artist Reuven Rubin

This museum occupies the former house of Reuven Rubin (1893–1974), one of Israel's pioneering modern artists. The architecture of the white stucco structure is typical of "Little Tel Aviv," as the neighborhoods of the 1920s are called. The permanent collection, of about 50 of Rubin's works, bequeathed to the museum by the artist, clearly illustrate the stages of his development.

Rubin, who was born in Rumania, studied painting in Jerusalem and Paris before settling in Tel Aviv in 1922. He derived his subjects from his surroundings: flowers, fruit trees, cityscapes, Arabs and Jews in native garb.

Girl with Dove *by Reuven Rubin*

Festivals, holidays, and biblical figures and events were also among his favorite themes. Over the years the naive yet vibrant quality of his early works gave way to a lyrical realism. Toward the end of his life, Rubin incorporated mystical elements into his work, as can be seen in such paintings as *Sukkot in Jerusalem* and *Abraham and the Three Angels*. Numerous realistic portraits and detailed drawings reveal Rubin's skill as a draftsman.

Rooster *by Reuven Rubin*

Most of the paintings are displayed on the ground floor of the house. On the second floor are Rubin's library, which is open to the public, and a biographical exhibit that highlights his achievements. A short audiovisual program about the painter's life and work is available in Hebrew and English. The artist's studio is on the third floor, with his brushes, palettes, and unfinished canvases as he left them.

HELENA RUBINSTEIN PAVILION

6 Tarsat Street, corner of Dizengoff Boulevard
Tel Aviv

HOURS: Sun.–Thurs. 10–22, Fri. 10–14,
       Sat. 10–14 and 19–22

TEL.: 03–299750
ADMISSION: $3.50
(includes admission to the Tel Aviv Museum of Art)

Focus: **Contemporary Art**

Adjacent to the Habimah Theater and the Mann Auditorium, the Helena Rubinstein Pavilion was the home of the Tel Aviv Museum of Art from 1959 to 1971. It is part of an impressive cultural complex in the center of Tel Aviv. The prominence of its location in the city is indicated by the very names of the two streets at the crossing: the T.R.S.T. of Tarsat Street stands for the Jewish calendar year 5669, equivalent to 1909, the year Tel Aviv was founded. The Dizengoff of Dizengoff Boulevard was the city's first mayor.

This pavilion, part of the Tel Aviv Museum of Art, houses loan exhibitions of both Israeli and international contemporary art. On permanent display is Helena Rubinstein's collection of miniature rooms. The exhibitions of contemporary art are listed in the calendar of the Tel Aviv Museum of Art and in the local newspapers.

TEL AVIV MUSEUM OF ART

27 Shaul Hamelech Boulevard
Tel Aviv

HOURS: Sun.–Thurs. 10–22, Fri. 10–14, Sat. 10–14 and 19–22   TEL.: 03–257361
ADMISSION: $3.50
Cafeteria on premises   (includes admission to the Helena Rubinstein Pavilion)

Focus: **Fine Arts**

The Tel Aviv Museum of Art is the largest museum in the country devoted solely to the fine arts. It opened originally in 1932 at the home of Meir Dizen-

Tel Aviv Museum of Art with Reclining Figure 1969–70 *by Henry Moore*

Solitude by Marc Chagall

goff, the city's first mayor; the current building, designed by Dan Eytan and Yitzhak Yashar, was inaugurated in 1971.

Entrance into the museum is from a spacious plaza in which several major sculptures are on view. The feeling of open space continues inside the museum—a welcome relief in a crowded city. In the vast central hall the ramp that leads up to the main exhibits forms a distinct geometric pattern: pillars, mobiles, and the changing daylight create their own kinetic shapes.

The Meyerhoff Pavilion exhibits Israeli art, beginning with the 1920s, when the countryside and its people were the main themes of the artists, who were for the most part newcomers to the landscape and often to the tradition of the fine arts. The later impressionistic movement known as "New Horizons" and the eclectic styles of the current Israeli art scene are also well represented. Yitzhak Danziger, Nahum Gutman, Menashe Kadishman, Moshe Kupferman, Reuven Rubin, and Yosef Zaritsky are but a few of the names encountered here.

Two of the museum's galleries house permanent collections of European and American art. These collections include works of the Old Masters, of Impressionists Renoir, Pissarro, Monet, and Van Gogh, and of such outstanding 20th-century artists as Picasso, Rouault, Klee, Kokoschka, Rothko, and Pollock. Of special note is an extensive selection of early works by Alexander Archipenko. The collections here have recently been enriched by the gift of more than 150 prints by Edvard Munch, which are shown on a rotating basis in a separate exhibition room.

The museum's Graphics Study Room, which contains over 15,000 prints and drawings, is open to the public for study and research. The German Expressionists are especially well represented. The museum's first director, art historian and collector Dr. Karl Schwarz, a native of Berlin, immigrated to Palestine in 1933 after the Nazis' rise to power and brought his collection to the museum, and he encouraged other German Jewish collectors to follow his example. Current holdings are extensive enough to make possible presentation of such thematic exhibits as "Five Centuries of Self-Portrait Prints" (May 1985), beginning with a print by Heinrich Aldegrever dating from 1537 and continuing through the works of Max Beckmann (1884–1950) and beyond.

The Tel Aviv Museum of Art has benefited from generous gifts by collectors and artists all over the world. In fact, the first canvas to enter its collection was a gift from Marc Chagall in 1931: his painting *Jew with Torah*. In 1979 the

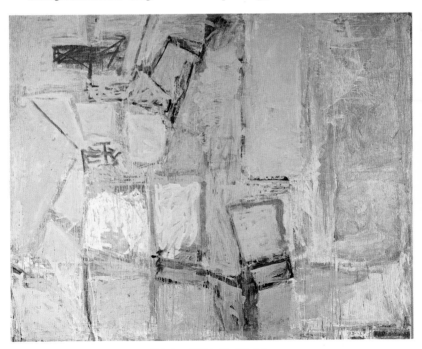

Painting, 1960 *by Josef Zaritsky*

museum acquired eleven gouaches by the Russian artist El Lissitsky painted as illustrations for "Had Gadya," a 16th-century song featured in the Passover Seder. On a visit to the Tel Aviv Museum in 1981, American artist Frank Stella was struck by the El Lissitsky gouaches and was inspired to begin work on a series of prints on the same theme. A gift to the museum added Stella's series, completed in 1984 and titled *Had Gadya After El Lissitsky*, to its collections. The El Lissitsky gouaches and the Stella hand-colored prints were first shown together in an exhibition at the museum in 1986.

The museum's paintings, sculptures, graphics, photography, and design are supplemented by imaginative programs of music, dance, theater, and film. Every evening but Friday the museum is open late, and usually a musical performance or other cultural event is held, either in the Recanati Auditorium or in the Kaufmann Hall. Not only regular appearances by the Tel Aviv

Jaffa Beach, 1926 *by Nahum Gutman*

Head, 1981 *by Menashe Kadishman*

Nude Seen from the Back *by Auguste Renoir*

Chamber Orchestra but rock concerts and even reggae music can be heard here. The Tel Aviv Museum of Art offers excellent art education classes and workshops for children and adults. (Newspapers carry complete listings.)

The Tel Aviv Museum of Art takes justifiable pride in serving as a showcase for young Israeli artists and in reflecting the latest trends on the Israeli art scene. "If the Israel Museum thinks of itself as the country's Metropolitan Museum," says Chief Curator Michael Levin, "perhaps we are its Museum of Modern Art."

This museum is one of the cultural treasures of Tel Aviv. For good measure, its gift shop, featuring an extensive selection of posters and catalogues, can provide unusual solutions to the problem of souvenirs.

THE THEATER MUSEUM
3 Melchett Street
Tel Aviv

HOURS: Mon.–Thurs. 9–14

TEL.: 03–292686
ADMISSION: Free

Focus: **Israeli and Jewish Theater**

This museum, primarily a theater archive, is located in an apartment in an old building in Tel Aviv. Its earliest documents—the records of a play performed at the Lemel School in Jerusalem—date from 1889. The collection is particularly rich in posters and sketches for set designs from the 1920s, when Hebrew theater and opera were coming into their own. There is also information relating to the theater companies of that era, such as Ohel, Li La Lo, Matateh, Kameri.

Exhibited separately is a selection of photographs and posters of 100 years of Yiddish theater, featuring such "wandering stars" as Maurice Schwartz and Ida Kaminska. And, chillingly, there is a program from Der Bergen-Belsener Dramatische Studiye.

The staff of this small archive-museum regards it as part of their function to assist interested students and visitors in making use of and enjoying the collection.

The Theater Museum is administered by the Eretz Israel Museum.

TEL AVIV ENVIRONS

BABYLONIAN JEWRY MUSEUM

Center for Iraqi Jewish Heritage
83 Hahagana Street
Or Yehuda

HOURS: Mon., Tues., Thurs. 9–12, Tues. 4–7 also   TEL.: 03–5369278
                                                    ADMISSION: Free

---

> By the rivers of Babylon,
> There we sat down, yea, we wept,
> When we remembered Zion.
> *Psalms 137:1*

The museum of the Jews of Babylonia charts and illumines the 2,500-year history of the Jews of Iraq. Together with the Center for Iraqi Jewish Heritage, of which it is part, the museum strives to preserve the distinctive lifestyle of the Jews of Iraq—their customs, liturgy, music, dress, and even cuisine—as well as to perpetuate their history. This history began when the rulers of Assyria and Babylon led captive into exile a large proportion of the population of the kingdoms of Israel and Judah (721–586 BC); it ended with the massive airborne transfer in 1950–51—known as "Operation Ezra and Nehemiah"—in which over 120,000 Jews were airlifted from Iraq to the newly founded State of Israel.

The museum's exhibits are grouped according to topic: Exile and Return, Settlement, Education, Leadership, and—as of the last 150 years—Jewish Communal Institutions, Zionism, and Immigration. Artifacts from the early centuries of the 2,500 years of Jewish life in Babylonia are rare, but the dramatic story is made real here through various viewer-activated displays. Pushing a button lights up a map so that the several routes into exile appear sequentially, in different colors. Another touch lights up the routes of the return of the Jews to Zion during the reign of King Cyrus in the 6th century BC, and of the exiles returning from Persia under the leadership of Ezra and Nehemiah a century later. Whenever a particular route lights up, so do the pertinent quotations, text panels, and graphics.

The history of the Jews who did not return to Zion in biblical times but remained on the banks of the Tigris and the Euphrates is clarified by other exhibits. After the destruction of Jerusalem by the Romans in AD 70, the Babylonian community began to occupy a central position in the world of Jewish learning, and its preeminence continued for centuries. Between the 7th and the 13th century, the *yeshivot* (schools for Talmudic study) of Sura, Pumbedita, and Nehadea, and their heads, the *geonim*, were especially influ-

---

Reconstruction of bimah *of the Great Synagogue of Baghdad*

ential. The main centers of learning, as well as the pattern of settlement, are shown in maps and dioramas. Two significant artifacts are a 5th-century clay incantation bowl and a 13th-century manuscript of the Babylonian Talmud.

The bulk of the material in the museum portrays the life of the Iraqi Jewish community in the 19th and 20th centuries. The major ceremonies marking events of the life cycle—birth, bar mitzvah, marriage, death—are represented handsomely. Clothes, jewels, charms, ritual objects, and other items are displayed against the background of photographs showing such objects in actual use. A large three-dimensional model of the Jewish Quarter in Baghdad testifies to the richness and diversity of the ancient community in its final years. Push-button lighting pinpoints the many institutions—medical centers, schools, *yeshivot*, synagogues, administrative centers, and others.

Life-cycle exhibit

Letters, pamphlets, newspaper clippings, documents, and photographs delineate the hardships suffered by the Jews of Iraq during the 1940s, a period of riots and persecutions. Their interest in Zionism and immigration to Palestine before 1948 are also well documented. A map traces the routes of "illegal" immigrants traveling to Palestine through Iran, Jordan, and even Saudi Arabia by camel, car, train, or plane—illegal because of the British restriction of the number of Jews admitted into the country. There are many photographs of the people airlifted in Operation Ezra and Nehemiah: lining up to register, in the planes, landing at Lod airport, traveling by truck to the *ma'abarot* (the primitive tent cities set up all over the new state to accommodate immigrants from the four corners of the earth).

The tour of the museum ends in a walk-through reconstruction of a Baghdad alley lined with small shops: a silversmith's, a weaver's, a cloth merchant's, a spice vendor's, a coffee shop—all with residential quarters on the second story. The alley leads to a model of the Great Synagogue of Baghdad, Selat Alkbigh; it is one-eighth the size of the original, except for the central wooden platform, the *bimah*, which is the same size as the original. The model is complete with Holy Ark, cabinets for additional Torahs (which held over 70 scrolls), and women's balconies. The synagogue, like the museum itself, is a testimony to the culturally rich life of the Jews of Iraq.

BEIT MIRIAM MUSEUM

Kibbutz Palmahim
Emek Sorek

HOURS: By appointment

TEL.: 03–965958
ADMISSION: Free

Focus: Archaeology of the Region

Beit Miriam Museum of Regional Antiquities

Archaeological exhibit

Travelers along the southern coastal road should certainly stop at Kibbutz Palmahim: the kibbutz is situated near the seashore and its museum is ideally located on a bluff overlooking a superb beach. If they are interested in archaeology, they will be especially well rewarded.

The archaeological collection contains some important artifacts, many of them from ancient burial sites found along the lower course of the nearby Nahal Sorek riverbed. From the Chalcolithic period come a bronze head of a goddess, clay statuettes of birds, and a unique ossuary in the shape of a round house. Also on display are skeletal material and tomb finds from the Late Bronze Age, as well as antiquities from the Persian and Hellenistic periods.

While some individual labels are in Hebrew only, each of the historical periods represented is identified in both Hebrew and English.

BEN ARI MUSEUM

2 Struma Street
Bat Yam

HOURS: Sun.–Thurs. 9–13 and 15:30–19	TEL: 03–868304
Fri. and Sat. 9–13	ADMISSION: Free

Focus: Contemporary Israeli Art

In its two-story circular building, this museum, located in a bustling town just south of Tel Aviv, offers exhibition opportunities to some of the less-well-known artists of Israel. It mounts a new show every other month. The exhibiting artist is invited to donate a work to the museum, and the permanent collection of the Ben Ari Museum is therefore growing rapidly.

This is a pleasant venue for viewing the current Israeli art scene. At times the works shown are unexpectedly eclectic: a recent exhibition of paintings by a Russian immigrant to Israel featured views of Leningrad.

MAN AND THE LIVING WORLD MUSEUM

Gan Leumi
Ramat Gan

HOURS: Sun.–Thurs. 9–14, Sat. 10–15	TEL.: 03–775509
	ADMISSION: $1.50

Focus: Participatory Exhibits of Basic Biological Concepts

Adjacent to the modern zoo in Ramat Gan's National Park, this museum is surrounded by flowering gardens with jacaranda, sycamore, and palm trees. Opened in 1983, it presents the story of biological evolution. A huge diorama entitled "Life 140 Million Years Ago" is a lifelike re-creation of dinosaurs and other extinct animals in their natural habitats. Other exhibits deal with animal locomotion, the human nervous system and brain, and vision. A display entitled "Reproduction and Genetics" shows the development of a baby and explains the role of DNA in human heredity.

The exhibits here are colorful and inviting, and some are participatory. "Touch Me" signs encourage children to make tactile contact with certain

Exhibit explaining DNA

displays. All labels, text panels, and instructions are clear and readable, in both Hebrew and English. For adults and for children over the age of ten this museum provides an intellectually stimulating and enjoyable experience.

Dinosaur exhibit

MISHKAN LE'OMANUT

31 Harzfeld Street
Holon

HOURS: Sun.–Thurs. 17–20, Sat. 10–13

TEL.: 03–882244
ADMISSION: Free

Focus: **Contemporary Israeli Art**

This well-lighted, modern-looking structure, built in 1936, was originally the home of Dr. Yehuda Meirov and his family. It was purchased by the municipality in 1960 and has since served as a public art museum.

Exhibits, which change monthly, consist of paintings by both emerging and well-established Israeli artists. The museum has acquired a small permanent collection of works through donations by the various artists who have exhibited here.

The museum's early evening hours have made it a popular meeting place for the residents of Holon, and the attendance figures are surprisingly high for a museum of this size.

MUSEUM OF ISRAELI ART

144 Abba Hillel Silver Street
Ramat Gan

HOURS: Sun.–Thurs. 9–21, Fri. 9–14, Sat. 10–16

TEL.: 03–7527377
ADMISSION: $2.00

Focus: **Painting, Sculpture, Photography, Graphics by Israeli Artists**

After several years of planning, this museum, devoted to exhibiting contemporary Israeli art, was opened in May 1987 by the municipality of Ramat Gan. Its first exhibition, titled "Big Format in Israeli Art," showed the works of many prominent artists, among them Benni Efrat, Pinchas Cohen Gan, Menashe Kadishman, Moshe Kupferman, Rafi Lavie, Joshua Neustein, and Igael Tumarkin. Director Meir Ahronson currently plans to stage a new loan exhibition every few months. The museum does not have a permanent collection.

The high-ceilinged galleries of the museum are ideal exhibition spaces. To create them, a 50-year-old former factory building was completely gutted and transformed.

HARRY OPPENHEIMER DIAMOND MUSEUM

1 Jabotinsky Street
Ramat Gan

HOURS: Sun., Mon., Wed., Thurs. 10–16, Tues. 10–19   TEL.: 03–214219
ADMISSION: Adults $2.00, children $1.00

Focus: **Israel's Diamond Industry**

Situated in the Diamond Exchange building, where Tel Aviv and Ramat Gan meet, this museum is a center of information about diamonds and other gems.

Diamond-polishing apparatus

A push-button model of the mining process illustrates the various extraction processes: crushing, washing, screening. The actual tools used in the process of polishing stones are also shown. A chart offers many facts and figures about the spectacular growth and development of the diamond industry in the country since its inception in 1936. Close to 10,000 workers are currently employed by the Israeli diamond industry, and the value of its annual export of polished gems far exceeds $1 billion. Two short films provide further information about the industry.

Reminding us of the association of beauty with holiness in the Bible is the museum's beautiful model of the *urim vetumim*, the breastplate worn by the high priest, made with twelve gems representing the tribes of Israel, in accordance with the biblical injunction "And thou shalt make a breastplate of judgment. . . . And thou shalt set in it settings of stones: . . . a row of carnelian, topaz, and smaragd . . . a carbuncle, a sapphire, and an emerald . . . a jacinth, an agate and an amethyst . . . a beryl, and an onyx, and a jasper; they shall be inclosed in gold in their settings" (Exodus 28:15–20). Large color transparencies of these gems are displayed throughout the museum.

RISHON LEZION HISTORY MUSEUM
4 Ahad Ha'am Street
Rishon Lezion

HOURS: Sun.–Thurs. 9–13 (Mon. and Wed. 16–19 also), Sat. 18–21   TEL.: 03–941621
ADMISSION: $3.00

Focus: **History of the Early Settlement**

This complex of several small houses tells the story of one of the earliest Jewish settlements in modern Palestine, founded in 1882 and named "First to Zion"—Rishon Lezion.

The story began when two of the founders, Zalman Levontin and Joseph Feinberg, with funds collected from investors, purchased 100 acres of land a few miles southeast of Jaffa and moved there with several families from Jerusalem. Among the settlers were members of Bilu, the association formed by young Jews in Russia who became the first Zionists to immigrate to Palestine (see Museum for the History of Gedera, page 240).

The first year was a disaster, for the harvest season was over by the time the new settlers had cleared the land and planted their crops. Intense heat,

Rishon Lezion History Museum

flies, Beduin attacks, and the shortage of water made matters worse. Some relief finally came, however, when with the help of Baron Edmond de Rothschild the settlers were able to drill a well. Soon the baron sent agronomists and supervisors to review the farming program, and at their suggestion vineyards were planted instead of grain. Still, one crisis followed another: the settlers complained that they were treated like hired help; the vines, imported from France, were not suitable; the wine produced could not compete in European markets. But with the baron's continued support, vine stocks improved, wine cellars were built, and Rishon Lezion began to produce the wine for which it is well known to this day.

The various rooms of the main house of the Rishon Lezion History Museum contain exhibits illustrating the early days of the settlement. In the entrance hall is an enlargement of a wonderfully descriptive photograph of the first seventeen families, some dressed in Eastern European garb, others in local costume, including the characteristic Turkish fez. Among them is Levontin, who many years later returned to Jerusalem to found the Anglo-Palestine Bank (see Bank Leumi Museum, page 84).

One of the rooms in the main house is labeled "Culture." Here there is a photograph of the first orchestra in the country, which was founded in Rishon

Lezion. The first Hebrew kindergarten and school were also established at this settlement, and another 19th-century photograph shows the principal standing beside Eliezer Ben-Yehuda, who single-mindedly fought for and won the acceptance of Hebrew as a modern spoken language. Text panels describe how teacher David Ydelovitch and all seven children in the school were given Hebrew names, including the only girl in the class. Photographs of famous visitors to Rishon Lezion, among them Theodor Herzl, Chaim Weizmann, Sir Herbert Samuel, and Albert Einstein, also grace this exhibit.

Elsewhere, in the small house that served as the settlement's original pharmacy, the early utensils and equipment used in the making and dispensing of medicines can be inspected.

Reconstructed street, with craftsman's workshop

The museum sponsors a walking tour to 13 historic sites in and around Founders Square, the center of the town. Highlights include the famous wine cellars, the community hall, and one of the first residences—a two-story building with a peaked roof reminiscent of Eastern European domestic architecture. The tour takes in, too, the still-functioning synagogue, which used to be called "the warehouse" because when it was built, in 1885, the Turkish authorities were willing to issue permits for such buildings but not for a house of worship.

Signs, labels, and text panels are mostly in Hebrew, but an English-speaking guide can be arranged for by calling in advance. Language should not be an obstacle to experiencing the historic and human interest of the Rishon Lezion History Museum.

RYBACK MUSEUM

6 Hadadi Street
Bat Yam

HOURS: Sun.–Thurs. 9–13 and 16–19 (Tues. 16–19),
Fri. 9–12, Sat. 9–13

TEL.: 03–868645
ADMISSION: Free

***Focus:* Paintings and Ceramics by Issachar Ryback**

Boy with a Goat *by Issachar Ryback*

The municipality of Bat Yam administers this small museum devoted to the artist Issachar Ryback (1897–1935). The collection of his work on permanent exhibition here was presented to Bat Yam by the artist's widow, Sonia, who served as the first director of the museum.

Born in the Ukraine, Issachar Ryback was early recognized as an artistic prodigy. He entered art school at the age of ten and won a scholarship to the prestigious Academy of Art in Kiev when only fourteen. In 1916—then nineteen—he went to Berlin to study and to paint. During his short life, Ryback's work was exhibited in many of the major cities of Europe. When he died, on the eve of the opening of his first one-man show in New York, Ryback was only thirty-eight.

Ryback's themes generally arise from remembrances of his youth. Many are somber childhood impressions of the pogroms—the wave of anti-Jewish violence that claimed his father's life. Ryback also worked in graphics and ceramics, and the museum owns a series of his ceramic figures representing characters from the *shtetl*.

Chamber music concerts are frequently held in the museum hall.

WEIZMANN MUSEUM
Weizmann Institute of Science
Hanasi Harishon Street
WEIZMANN HOUSE
Herzl Street
Rehovot

HOURS: Sun.–Thurs. 10–15:30

TEL.: 08–473960 or 08–483230
ADMISSION: Museum, free
House, $1.50

Focus: **Chaim Weizmann, Israel's First President**

In a large gallery on the ground floor of the Wix Library, visitors to the Weizmann Institute can learn about and ponder on the life and career of Chaim Weizmann, renowned scientist and first president of the State of Israel. Memorabilia exhibited here include his diploma from Fribourg University in Switzerland, from which he was graduated magna cum laude in 1899, and various items of scientific equipment, among them the incubator that he used for microbiological studies in his research laboratory in London in the 1930s. In this museum there are also letters, postcards, documents, and photographs chronicling Weizmann's life and his crucial role in Zionist politics. A historic

Interior, Weizmann House, Rehovot

photograph shows Weizmann, Theodor Herzl, and Martin Buber at the Fifth Zionist Congress in Basel, in 1901.

About half a mile away from the library is the house, designed by architect Eric Mendelsohn, where Chaim and Vera Weizmann established their residence in 1937. A tape-recorded tour is available at any time; if enough visitors are present, a guided tour is offered every 30 minutes.

The interior of the house remains as it was when the Weizmanns lived there, with its beautiful Oriental rugs and fine paintings by Israeli and foreign artists. There is also a photograph gallery of the world figures whom Weizmann knew and worked with. Among the family pictures is a photograph of the Weizmanns' youngest son, killed in World War II.

Weizmann House

From the garden surrounding the Weizmann house there is a scenic view: "Judea and the valley belong to the house," the architect wrote. In the garden, on the slope facing to the east, toward Jerusalem, are the graves of Chaim and Vera Weizmann.

YAD LEBANIM MUSEUM

Wolfson Street
Herzliya

HOURS: Sun.–Thurs. 16–20, Sat. 10–13

TEL.: 052–551011
ADMISSION: Free

Focus: Contemporary Israeli Art

Founded in 1964 in memory of the young men of Herzliya who lost their lives in Israel's wars (*Yad Lebanim* means "Memorial to the Sons"), this museum moved in 1975 to its present location, a building designed by Israeli architect Yaacov Rechter.

On view here are the works of contemporary Israeli painters and sculptors; exhibits change every two to three months. As is customary with many small art museums in Israel, the permanent collection is gradually being enlarged by works donated by exhibiting artists.

One of the small galleries in the museum is devoted to the work of South African–born sculptor Lippy Lipshitz.

YAD LEBANIM MUSEUM

30 Arlozorov Street
Petah Tikva

HOURS: Mon.–Thurs. 16:30–19:30, Sat. 10–13

TEL: 03–9223450
ADMISSION: Free

***Focus:* Petah Tikva's History; Memorial to the Town's Fallen Soldiers; Regional Archaeology; Israeli Art**

This museum, founded in 1951 by Petah Tikva as a memorial to the young men of the town who had fallen in the 1948 War, has since become a prototype for many other such memorials in the country. Set in a beautiful park, it comprises four exhibition pavilions and also a library and archives.

The museum's central memorial hall contains several rooms, one dedicated to the Unknown Soldier and another to the theme "Flowers and Peace." Photographs, diaries, documents, small arms, and other memorabilia from Israel's wars are exhibited, and the names of the fallen soldiers are engraved on the walls.

Petah Tikva *by Zvi Shor*

The art pavilion, considered to be one of the leading small showcases for art in Israel, features both permanent and changing exhibits of contemporary Israeli art. It often mounts retrospective shows of the work of well-known

Jerusalem *by Mordechai Levanon*

Israeli painters and sculptors, yet it also provides exhibition space for younger artists.

The archaeological pavilion displays many artifacts excavated at nearby Tel Aphek, site of the ancient city of Aphek, which was established in the Early Bronze Age, approximately 5,000 years ago. Strategically located near the sources of the Yarkon River, it was an important administrative and commercial center on the *via maris*, the ancient "Way of the Sea," which connected Egypt and Mesopotamia. Aphek is mentioned in the Bible as having been conquered by Joshua and, later, by the Philistines (Joshua 12:18, 19; I Samuel 4:1). In the 1st century BC, Herod the Great rebuilt the city and renamed it Antipatris, in honor of his father, Antipater. More than 1,000 years later the Crusaders fortified the site, as did the Ottoman Turks in the 16th century. Characteristic artifacts from all these historical periods—including tools, pottery vessels, lamps, scarabs, seals, and coins—are to be seen here.

The fourth of this museum's major pavilions is devoted to the history of

The War of Independence *by Zvi Gali*

Petah Tikva, renowned as the first Jewish agricultural settlement of modern times. Designated as *em hamoshavot*, "mother of the settlements," it was founded in 1878, several years before the arrival of the first Zionist pioneers from Europe. The name Petah Tikva (Door of Hope) is from Hosea 2:17. Historical documents, agricultural implements, building tools, arms, and other memorabilia are reminders of the hard work and the difficulties faced by the settlement's *meyasdim*, or founders, who left the relative safety of Jerusalem and moved here with the ideal of becoming self-sufficient farmers who would not have to depend on charity from abroad. The exhibits tell of the many obstacles these early settlers had to overcome, including their own lack of experience, hostility from the surrounding population, and the threat of disease posed by the malarial swamps nearby.

The museum's library and archives specialize in subjects relating to the history of Petah Tikva: books, letters, documents, clippings, and other items dating from the town's early days to the mid-1940s.

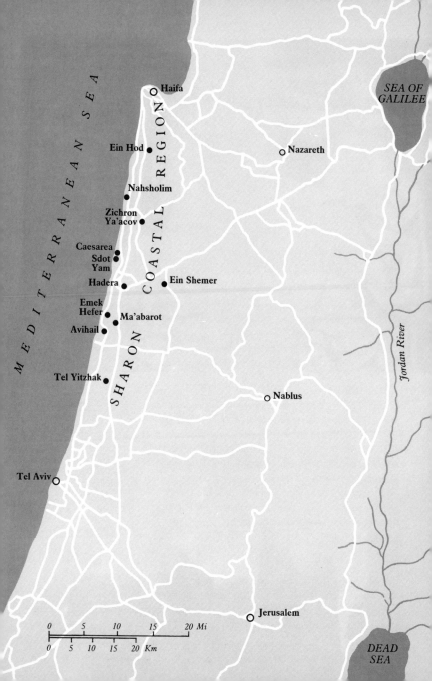

SHARON COASTAL REGION

BEIT AARONSOHN

40 Hameyasdim Street
Zichron Ya'acov

HOURS: Sun.–Thurs. 9:30–13

TEL.: 06–390120
ADMISSION: $1.50

Focus: **Nili, the World War I Jewish Underground**

The modern museum building and the late-19th-century house nearby are dedicated to the memory of the Aaronsohn family. The parents, who were among the founders of this vintners' village, arrived in Palestine in 1882. Their eldest son, Aaron, became a noted agronomist, famous for his discovery of *Triticum dicoccoides*, the ancestor of modern wheat. Even more dramatic was the phase of his career that began during World War I: together with his sister, Sara, and his brother, Alexander, he organized an underground movement to help liberate Palestine from Ottoman rule by passing military secrets to British intelligence in Cairo and London. The group called itself Nili, an acronym of the biblical words "the Glory of Israel will not lie" (I Samuel 15:29).

The museum's collection of letters, photographs, diaries, and other documents tells the story. In the spring of 1917, Sara Aaronsohn traveled through Anatolia and Syria gathering information on the Turkish army. On her return to Zichron Ya'acov, she, her father, and several other members of Nili were arrested by the Turks. To spare the others, Sara took full responsibility for the espionage activities. Although tortured for four days, she revealed nothing. Before being transported to a prison in Nazareth she asked if she could bathe and change her clothes in Aaron's house, and here, with a gun that had been smuggled in to her, she took her own life. Aaron survived the war but was killed in a plane crash in 1919, on his way to promote the Zionist cause at the Paris Peace Conference.

Aaron's house is preserved as it was during World War I, with its library, family photographs, and decor of Oriental rugs and French and Turkish furniture. The rest of Zichron Ya'acov is well worth exploring. Its central square, overlooking the Carmel hills and the Mediterranean, has changed little since its founding in the 1880s and retains its picturesque small-town character.

BEIT HAGEDUDIM
Avihail

HOURS: Sun.–Thurs. 8:30–14, Fri. 8:30–13	TEL.: 053–22212
Cafeteria on premises	ADMISSION: $1.00

Focus: Zion Mule Corps and Jewish Battalions in World War I

In Beit Hagedudim (House of the Battalions) the subject matter is the establishment of Jewish military units within the British Army in World War I and their role in the victorious Palestine campaign. Composed of volunteers from Great Britain, the United States, Australia, and Canada—as well as individuals expelled from Palestine by the Ottomans—these units constituted the first organized Jewish military force since the time of the Bar Kokhba revolt of AD 132–35.

The permanent exhibits at Beit Hagedudim picture the early days of the battalions, beginning with the creation of the Zion Mule Corps in Alexandria

Portico with busts of Jabotinsky and Trumpeldor

by Ze'ev (Vladimir) Jabotinsky, founder of Zionist Revisionism (see Jabotinsky Institute, page 96), and Joseph Trumpeldor, a former Russian army officer who became a military leader among the Jewish settlers in Palestine (see Tel Hai Museum, page 208).

A brief audiovisual presentation recalls the disastrous Allied attempt at landing at Gallipoli in 1915 and details the part played by the Zion Mule Corps. Many members of the corps were killed or wounded in this bloody and futile campaign.

Photographs, documents, and military memorabilia illustrate the subsequent role of the Jewish units in the British invasion of Palestine, starting in 1917 with the formation of the 38th, 39th, and 40th Royal Fusiliers Battalions, into which the Jewish volunteer units were organized. Among the Zionist leaders who served in these forces were David Ben-Gurion, who became the first prime minister of Israel, and Yitzhak Ben Zvi, Israel's second president. It is likewise of historic interest to follow the story of Eliezer Margolin of

Rehovot, who, seeking a better livelihood, had emigrated to Australia but, with the outbreak of World War I, answered the call for volunteers and eventually became the commander of the 39th Battalion.

Their actual uniforms, medals, and swords, together with many photographs and documents, summon up remembrance of the battalions' commanders. Among them was Colonel John Patterson, first commander of the Zion Mule Corps, who later served as commander of the 38th Battalion. The establishment of Magen David Adom, the first-aid organization (corresponding to the Red Cross) attached to the Jewish Battalions, the surrender of Jerusalem to the British in 1917, and the appointment of Sir Herbert Samuel as first high commissioner in Palestine are other events evoked here.

Finally, a significant display describes how the Jewish volunteers who remained in Palestine organized themselves into a single battalion called "The First Judeans," and how many of them later performed key roles in the Jewish underground, which eventually became the nucleus of the Israel Defense Forces.

Beit Hagedudim, designed by Hanna and Nathan Golani, was built in 1958. Avihail was chosen to be the site of the museum because the settlement was established by former members of the battalions.

Members of the Zion Mule Corps

CAESAREA MUSEUM/BEIT HANNA SENNESH

Kibbutz Sdot Yam

HOURS: Sun.–Fri. 9–12, Sat. 10–12 (or by appointment) TEL.: 06–364367
ADMISSION: Free

Focus: **Archaeological Finds from Caesarea, Mostly Roman and Byzantine**

Courtyard of Caesarea Museum/Beit Hanna Sennesh

This museum in Kibbutz Sdot Yam is located just a few hundred yards south of the site of the ancient city of Caesarea, built by Herod the Great at the end of the 1st century BC. The city later served as a provincial Roman capital; during the Byzantine period it was the seat of a bishop and a center of Christian learning. Its spectacular archaeological remains, including a restored Roman theater and massive Crusader fortifications and harbor works, make it one of the most interesting sites in Israel.

The Caesarea Museum houses a fine collection of Roman statuary, ancient coins issued at Caesarea, clay lamps from Roman and Byzantine times, finds from a 5th-century synagogue, and a group of ancient tombstones with Greek, Latin, and Hebrew inscriptions.

Founded by kibbutz member Aharon Wegman, the museum began with a small collection comprising artifacts that were on the ground or were turned up by plowing in the surrounding agricultural fields in the 1940s. Unexpected discoveries in this area have continued. During the construction of a new

Roman theater   *Following pages: Crusader wall in harbor of Caesarea*

factory for the kibbutz, workers came upon two large marble statues placed at what appears to have been the southern gate to the city in Byzantine times.

The museum was named in memory of Hanna Sennesh, a young member of the kibbutz who was parachuted behind enemy lines during World War II in a joint effort by the Haganah and the British army to gather information and to organize Jewish resistance in occupied Europe. Sennesh was captured in Budapest and tortured and executed by the Gestapo. She was twenty-three years old.

EMEK HEFER REGIONAL MUSEUM
Ruppin Institute
Emek Hefer

HOURS: Sun.–Fri. 8:30–13:30

TEL.: 053–688644
ADMISSION: $1.50

Focus: **Archaeology and Natural History of the Region**

The Emek Hefer Regional Museum, opened in 1959, is an educational institute for local schoolchildren, from kindergarten through high school, some 30,000 of whom visit this complex of buildings annually. Individual visitors and families are also welcomed.

The museum's exhibits of prehistoric archaeology feature dioramas and reconstructed sites as backgrounds for artifacts found in the surrounding countryside. Special emphasis is placed on the life-style of early humans as hunters, food-gatherers, and toolmakers. Young visitors are encouraged to handle prehistoric stone tools, which are displayed in open cases.

An actual-size reconstruction of a Chalcolithic burial cave contains authentic ossuaries, incense burners, and jars excavated nearby. There is also a large-scale model of a tell, an ancient mound, showing in cross section a typical Canaanite house.

The nature museum is in a separate building. Here a fine collection of indigenous animals and waterfowl are seen to disport in their natural habitats in large dioramas of the seashore, marshlands, and streams. This section houses extensive collections of butterflies and insects from all over the world and reptiles from the region.

The labels are in Hebrew (with Latin zoological terms), but most exhibits are self-explanatory.

This museum has many attractions for families with young children.

HATZAR HARISHONIM

Kibbutz Ein Shemer

HOURS: Sun.–Thurs. 8–16, Fri. 8–12, Sat. 8–16   TEL.: 06–374327
Café nearby   ADMISSION: $2.00

Focus: History of the Kibbutz

This complex, which opened in 1988 to mark the 60th anniversary of the founding of Ein Shemer, comprises the original buildings of the kibbutz—a quadrangle known as Hatzar Harishonim (The Courtyard of the Pioneers). The museum building, situated at the entrance to the quadrangle, is devoted to "Ein Shemer, Past and Present." One section contains archaeological discoveries excavated nearby—pottery and glass vessels, jewelry and coins—and specimens of the flora and fauna of the region. The main displays stress the development of the kibbutz over the past 60 years, utilizing photographs, maps, and other documents. The audiovisual program is a good introduction to a tour of the restored buildings.

Members of the kibbutz have assembled outdoor exhibits of agricultural machinery—harvesters, balers, combines, and tractors—some of which can be activated by pressing a button. Farm equipment from the earliest days of the kibbutz is preserved in the old silo, alongside exhibits dealing with grain, bread, and baking. The stables, the blacksmith's shop, and the other workshops have been returned to their original condition, as has the first dining room of the kibbutz, where mannequins sit around the tables.

*Courtyard
of the
Pioneers*

JANCO–DADA MUSEUM
Ein Hod

HOURS: Sun.–Thurs. 9:30–17, Fri. 9:30–16, Sat. 9:30–17
Café across the street

TEL.: 04–842350
ADMISSION: $1.50

Focus: Art of Marcel Janco

Janco–Dada Museum and artists' village of Ein Hod

Located on the western slopes of Mount Carmel, in the artists' village of Ein Hod, this museum features the works of Marcel Janco (1895–1984), the village's founder, who was a member of the small group that launched the Dada art movement of the early decades of the 20th century. On view are examples of Janco's work throughout his career: his youth in Rumania, his middle years in Zurich and Paris, the period after his arrival in Palestine, in 1941, and the years after his founding of Ein Hod, in 1953.

Emphasis is on Janco's participation in the Dada movement and on his contributions to the development of contemporary Israeli art. The museum's collection spans 70 years, and all the mediums and genres Janco experimented with are represented: collages, drawings, portraits, landscapes, historic

Party *by Marcel Janco*

themes, and abstract compositions. An informative slide show of Janco and his work, narrated currently only in Hebrew, is presented. Labels and text panels are in both Hebrew and English.

The museum mounts about four exhibitions each year, and its small shop has attractive calendars and catalogues for sale. Visitors are urged to explore the surrounding village of Ein Hod—whose name means "Spring of Splendor"—and are welcomed at the studios and workshops of the resident artists, where paintings, sculptures, ceramics, prints, and weaving are on view.

KHAN HISTORICAL MUSEUM

74 Hagiborim Street
Hadera

HOURS: Sun.–Thurs. 8:30–13 (Tues. 16–18 also), Fri. 9–12   TEL.: 06–322330
ADMISSION: $2.00

Focus: **Settlement of Hadera**

Courtyard with artifacts

Located in an old Ottoman *khan*, a caravanserai that once sheltered traders and their camel caravans, this museum recalls the early history of Jewish settlers in Hadera and their way of life. The story began in 1891, with the arrival in Jaffa of four Jewish immigrants from czarist Russia who hoped to purchase land on which they and their families could settle.

With Yehoshua Hankin, a land dealer and active supporter of Zionist colonization, the four traveled north to look over an available tract of some 17,500 acres. Although the prospective settlers noticed the jaundiced complexion of the local Beduin, they did not suspect that these deceptively green acres were swampland, plagued with malaria. They purchased the land and named their new home Hadera, from the Arabic *hudair* ("green"). Soon they wrote to their families in Russia: "Sell out and come over here. The land is good, water plentiful. We'll be able to raise fish. There is a wonderful seashore. The land is arable and there is even a place to live in, a 26 room building [the *khan*] which we have already begun to clean up and renovate."

Of the first wave of 540 pioneers, 210 died in the first two decades. Yet throughout those terrible years of illness and financial hardship, the settlers of Hadera continued to labor untiringly to drain the swamps and establish themselves as farmers. By 1910, life became more tolerable. New houses were built, and, after successive failures, agricultural methods improved.

The *khan*, the first building occupied by the settlers, has been restored to its appearance in the late 19th century; typical of that era are the decorated tile floors. On view are household goods, furniture, and agricultural and other implements used by the newcomers, including an oil press. Photographs show the settlers draining the swamps with the help of water buffalo and planting eucalyptus trees. The development of the local citrus industry is glimpsed in pictures of crates of oranges being carried by camels to Jaffa.

The museum also features a slide show that documents Hadera's history, and it has a library that specializes in the history of modern Jewish settlement in Palestine.

MA'ABAROT MUSEUM
Kibbutz Ma'abarot

HOURS: By appointment

TEL.: 053–82889
ADMISSION: Free

Focus: Local Archaeological Finds

This small museum, maintained by the members of Kibbutz Ma'abarot, houses locally excavated archaeological finds, including flint implements, weapons, and coins. Most impressive is a Middle Bronze Age burial cave discovered during the construction of the museum building. Here the bones, weapons, and pottery vessels can be seen in situ, as they were found.

MASSUAH HOLOCAUST POST MUSEUM
Kibbutz Tel Yitzhak

HOURS: By appointment

TEL.: 053–99997
ADMISSION: Free

Focus: Letters from the Time of the Holocaust

Within a large concrete building in Kibbutz Tel Yitzhak is a museum that houses letters, postcards, stamps, and other items sent through the mails during the Holocaust. The collection is constantly expanding as the purpose of the museum becomes known. Texts and labels are currently only in Hebrew. Lectures and seminars relating to the collection are held in the building's auditorium and classrooms.

NAHSHOLIM MUSEUM

Kibbutz Nahsholim
Hof Dor

HOURS: Daily 9–13

TEL.: 06–390950
ADMISSION: $1.50

Focus: **Archaeology of Tel Dor and Its Harbor**

Nahsholim Museum ("The Glass Factory")

Situated halfway between Tel Aviv and Haifa, on one of Israel's loveliest beaches, Kibbutz Nahsholim's museum is devoted to regional and underwater archaeology. The museum occupies a century-old glass factory originally built by Baron Edmond de Rothschild to provide bottles for the developing wine industry at nearby Zichron Ya'acov. Unfortunately the local sand yielded unattractive black glass, and the factory building was abandoned within two years of its construction. Its recent restoration and transformation into a museum are largely due to the efforts of Kurt Raveh, a Dutch-born member of Kibbutz Nahsholim who is one of the pioneers of underwater archaeology in Israel.

The museum presents frequent lectures and films to further general appreciation of the archaeological treasures that lie beneath the sea. Lining the entrance corridor is an array of stone anchors—some dating from the Bronze Age—which were retrieved from the nearby bay. Other underwater finds include 14th-century BC pottery from a sunken Canaanite vessel, a group of Persian-period statuettes, clay figurines of the goddess Astarte—one with the mold from which it was cast—and pottery and other objects from a "modern" wreck of 1661. Also noteworthy are four flintlock muskets, a portion of a sword, a scabbard, and a five-foot bronze cannon lost at sea when one of Napoleon's boats sank in 1799, during his Middle Eastern campaign.

Ancient anchors

The museum's collection includes finds from the ongoing excavations at nearby Tel Dor, site of the ancient city of Dor mentioned in the Bible (Judges 1:27) and in Egyptian and Assyrian records. In the 12th century BC, Dor was settled by the Sea Peoples, associated with the Philistines, and it continued to serve as a port city and a fortress through the Hellenistic, Roman, and Byzantine periods. All these periods are represented among the finds.

An opportunity to visit Tel Dor—and even to participate in the excavations—is offered to visitors staying at the guest house of Kibbutz Nahsholim during the annual digging season, generally from June to August.

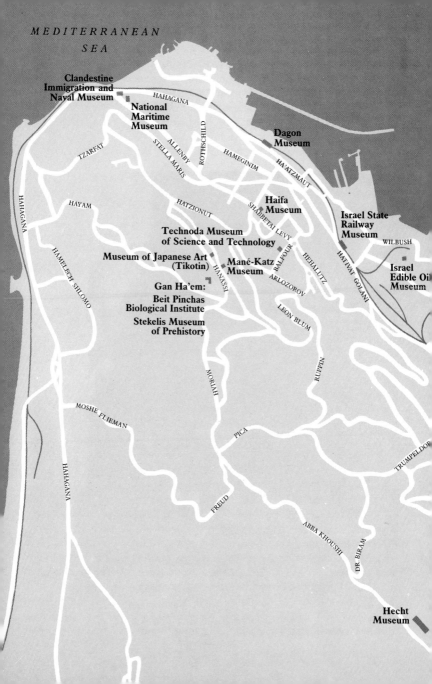

MEDITERRANEAN SEA

Clandestine
Immigration and
Naval Museum

HAHAGANA

National
Maritime
Museum

TZARFAT

ALLENBY

STELLA MARIS

ROTHSCHILD

HAMEGINIM

Dagon
Museum

HA'ATZMAUT

HAYAM

HATZIONUT

Haifa
Museum

SHABBETAI LEVY

Israel State
Railway
Museum

WILBUSH

HAMELECH SHLOMO

Technoda Museum
of Science and Technology

Museum of Japanese Art
(Tikotin)

HANASSI

Mané-Katz
Museum

BALFOUR

ARLOZOROV

HEHALUTZ

HATIVAT GOLANI

Israel
Edible Oil
Museum

Gan Ha'em:
Beit Pinchas
Biological Institute

Stekelis Museum
of Prehistory

LEON BLUM

HAHAGANA

MORIAH

RUPPIN

MOSHE FLIEMAN

PICA

TRUMPELDOR

HAHAGANA

FREUD

ABBA KHOUSHI

DR. BIRAM

Hecht
Museum

HAIFA

CLANDESTINE IMMIGRATION
AND NAVAL MUSEUM

204 Allenby Road
Haifa

HOURS: Sun.–Thurs. 9–15, Fri. 9–12

TEL.: 04–536249
ADMISSION: $1.00

Focus: **Clandestine Immigration to Palestine**

Illegal immigration ship Af-al-pi-chen

Overlooking Haifa Bay, this museum has two themes, both related to the sea. Before reaching the museum's main section, which is devoted to *ha'apala* (clandestine immigration), visitors can tour the Naval Exhibition, where the history of Israel's navy is recorded in displays that include ship models, naval memorabilia, maps, charts, and photographs. Noteworthy are a scale model of the Egyptian battleship *Ibrahim al-Awal*, captured in 1956, and a buoy from the *Dakar*, the Israeli submarine lost at sea in 1968.

The Clandestine Immigration exhibits chronicle the events of the period between 1934 and the establishment of the State of Israel in 1948, during which some 125,000 "illegal" Jewish immigrants made their way into Palestine by means of covert sea voyages and overland convoys. This movement was particularly intense after World War II, which left hundreds of thousands of displaced persons, survivors of the Holocaust, homeless in Europe. Because the British, pressured by Arab demands to restrict Jewish immigration, allowed only a trickle of refugees to enter Palestine, the Jewish leadership organized a major attempt to run the British naval blockade.

A large map illustrates the land and sea routes taken by the refugees. Documents, photographs, and actual fragments of vessels speak volumes about rescue episodes, details of deportation, the sinking of ships, and the courage of those who helped the refugees. Photomurals show some of the ships used, the most famous of which was the *Exodus*, intercepted 12 miles outside Palestine's territorial waters. Its 4,530 passengers fought valiantly to evade arrest until the British forces opened fire, killing 3 passengers and wounding 100. The crew finally surrendered when the British threatened to ram the ship and sink it. Badly damaged, the *Exodus* was towed into Haifa harbor, where the refugees were transferred to another vessel and sent back to Germany.

Also part of the tragic saga of clandestine immigration is the SS *Struma*, which, with over 700 Jewish refugees from Nazi Germany on board, limped into Istanbul harbor in December of 1941, its crew hoping to make the necessary repairs and continue the voyage. But the Turks, informed by the British that the ship would not be allowed to land in Palestine, refused to assist them. The *Struma* remained in the harbor for two months, its passengers suffering from hunger and disease, until the Turks finally towed it out to sea. The ship subsequently sank, and all 428 men, 269 women, and 70 children aboard perished.

The centerpiece of the museum is one of the illegal ships, *Af-al-pi-chen*, whose Hebrew name means "in spite of" or "nevertheless." Visitors can board the small ship from the roof of the museum and enter the cramped fore section, where its 434 refugee passengers slept during a Mediterranean crossing in 1947.

Between the end of World War II and 1948, all but 5 of the 63 clandestine immigration ships were intercepted by British naval forces, and 26,000 refugees were deported to overcrowded camps in Cyprus ominously reminiscent, with their barbed-wire fences, searchlights, and armored-car patrols, of the concentration camps from which they had just been liberated. The last of the deportees interned on Cyprus were finally brought to Israel in February 1949.

A tour of this museum is a moving and enlightening experience, inspiring renewed appreciation of the role of the organizations in charge of the clandestine immigration in saving lives and in helping to bring about the establishment of the State of Israel. All labels here are in both Hebrew and English, and introductory brochures as well as detailed guides to the exhibits are available on request at the entrance.

DAGON MUSEUM

Plumer Square
Haifa

HOURS: Guided tours are conducted Sun.–Fri. from 10:30 on. The museum is not open to the public at other times, but group tours can be arranged by appointment.

TEL.: 04–664221
ADMISSION: Free

Focus: **History of Grain**

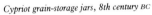
Cypriot grain-storage jars, 8th century BC

Clay figurine of baker kneading dough,
3rd century BC

While there are several museums in the world dealing with bread, the Dagon Museum is the only one devoted to the subject of grain—its cultivation, handling, storage, and distribution, and its cultural significance from the Neolithic period to the present. Located at the foot of the Dagon silo, which is equipped for the handling yearly of hundreds of thousands of tons of grain, soybeans, and other crops, the museum covers the history of growing cereals—their varieties and their utilization in the land of Israel and in neighboring countries. Archaeological artifacts displayed here were donated by Dr. Reuben Hecht, chairman and director of the Dagon silo complex.

Exhibits include 4,000-year-old grains of wheat, bone sickle handles, ancient Egyptian murals, wooden models of Egyptian silos, clay statues of bread bakers from the Hellenistic period, ostraca (potsherds with inscriptions) describing the distribution of grain, fertility goddesses, coins depicting grain, bread stamps, and Early Iron Age beer jugs with specially made strainer spouts for the pouring of a coarse barley brew.

The 215-foot Dagon silo dominates the skyline of downtown Haifa, and the museum is easily located. Trained volunteer guides, many of whom are employees of the Dagon silo complex, are on hand to give explanations. Exhibits are well-lighted and are labeled in both Hebrew and English.

GAN HA'EM MUSEUMS
Beit Pinchas Biological Institute
124 Hatishbi Street, Mount Carmel
Haifa

HOURS: Sun.–Thurs. 8–16, Sat. 9–16
    (reptile collection closed on Sun.)

TEL.: 04–337886 or 04–337390
ADMISSION: $4.00

Stekelis Museum of Prehistory

HOURS: Sun.–Thurs. 8–14, Sat. 10–14
Refreshments available at kiosk on premises

TEL.: 04–337833
ADMISSION: $.75

Focus: **Botanical Gardens; Zoo; History of Early Mankind**

Exhibit at Stekelis Museum of Prehistory

Gan Ha'em, or "Mother's Park," is situated on the slopes of Mount Carmel, with a sweeping view of the Mediterranean. Within its extensive, sprawling grounds are a botanical garden, a small nature museum, a zoo, and a museum of prehistory. This multifaceted park is the realization of the lifelong dream of Pinchas Cohen, educator and nature lover.

The botanical garden, set within the lush natural surroundings of a flowing stream, Nahal Lotem, features the indigenous flora of the Carmel and Galilee regions. Rare species of mosses, ferns, and hydrophils thrive here in the orbit of a man-made waterfall.

Among the live animals housed in the zoo are deer, lions, monkeys, waterfowl, and birds of prey. Its live reptile collection, one of the largest in Israel, includes snakes and lizards native to the country as well as boas, pythons, cobras, vipers, and rattlesnakes from all over the world. The nearby nature museum is devoted to local fauna; its displays include mounted mammals, birds, and fish.

The Museum of Prehistory was founded in 1961 by Professor Moshe Stekelis of the Hebrew University. Many of the finds on view here were discovered at sites throughout the Carmel Range, which extends southward from Haifa along the Mediterranean coast. Dioramas re-create scenes in the daily life of Stone Age hunters and of the earliest farmers, in the Neolithic period. The culture of the period of transition from hunting to farming is illustrated by a model of a Natufian village (c. 10,000 BC) and a reconstructed Natufian burial site with its carefully interred skeletons, seashell ornaments, and stone tools.

Gan Ha'em—the park itself—is open all week, and it is a pleasant place in which to relax and enjoy the scenery. Its various museum facilities attract an interesting mix of Israeli and foreign visitors.

HAIFA MUSEUM
Museum of Ancient Art
Museum of Modern Art
Museum of Music and Ethnography
26 Shabbetai Levy Street
Haifa

HOURS: Sun.–Thurs. and Sat. 10–13
(Tues., Thurs., Sat. 18–21 also)

TEL.: 04–523255
ADMISSION: $2.50

Focus: Ancient and Modern Art; Music and Ethnography

Three separate museums, housed within a single structure, make up the Haifa Museum. Space is understandably at a premium and plans are being formulated by the municipality of Haifa, which administers the museums, to transfer them to a larger facility when funds become available.

The Museum of Ancient Art, founded in 1949 and based on the private collection of Dr. Alexander Roche, specializes in aesthetically pleasing ar-

Fayyum portrait on wood

chaeological finds discovered in Israel and the Mediterranean basin. From Greece come marble statues and painted vases; from ancient Egypt come a collection of burial masks and other funerary objects, Roman-period portraits from the Fayyum, and Coptic textiles. The Eastern Mediterranean is represented by a selection of terra-cotta figurines from the 1st millennium BC and a comprehensive collection of coins issued in Acre and Caesarea. Occasional temporary exhibits feature finds from the archaeological excavations at Shik-

Coptic textile

Mosaic floor from 6th-century church at Shikmona

mona, situated on the southern outskirts of Haifa, which was occupied from the Middle Bronze Age to the Byzantine period. Exceptionally beautiful mosaic floors were found in a 6th-century church at the site. All labels in the Museum of Ancient Art are in English and Hebrew; clear and detailed text panels provide even a novice with a broad overview of the exhibits.

The Museum of Modern Art, founded in 1951, exhibits works from all over the world, ranging in date from the mid-18th century to the present. It prides itself on its collection of 20th-century graphics and contemporary Israeli paintings, sculptures, crafts, and photography. Solo shows of artists from abroad are frequently held, as are exhibits on thematic topics, for example, "Young Artists from West Berlin" and "Art Posters from Britain and the United States."

A small section of the building houses the Museum of Music and Ethnography. Featured here on a rotating basis are folk music instruments from five continents and expertly crafted reproductions of musical instruments known from the Bible and used in the lands of the ancient Near East. The ethnographical displays include embroideries, domestic utensils, and tools from many countries. Typical costumes from Jewish communities in the Diaspora, as well as those worn by the Arab and Druze communities near Haifa, are also shown. An impressive collection of jewelry exemplifies the work of Jewish silversmiths around the world.

All three museums have fine libraries and offer special services to the public; interested visitors should call for further information.

REUBEN AND EDITH HECHT MUSEUM

Main Building, University of Haifa
Mount Carmel
Haifa

HOURS: Sun.–Thurs. 10–17, Sat. 10–13

TEL.: 04–240577
ADMISSION: Free

Focus: The People of Israel in the Land of Israel

In the modern tower building of the University of Haifa, located at the top of Mount Carmel, the Reuben and Edith Hecht Museum was opened to the public in 1984. Its permanent exhibits, based on the collection of Dr. Reuben Hecht, are arranged chronologically from the Chalcolithic through the Byzantine period, with strong emphasis on the Israelite period.

Religious and cult objects such as altars, lamps, and figurines are exhibited in a long entrance hall that also features photomurals of ancient temples with the same time horizons as the objects shown. The main gallery is spacious and well-lighted; its handsome display cases enhance the visual impact of the ancient artifacts. Extensive texts and labels accompany these well-designed exhibits.

Ivory cosmetics box in shape of duck, mid-2nd millennium BC

Terra-cotta head with traces of paint

Noteworthy among the objects shown here are a group of miniature figurines of sheep, cattle, and other animals from the Early Bronze Age and, from the Middle Bronze Age, an ostrich egg fashioned into a vessel by the addition of a neck and bronze handles. Two anthropoid coffins from the 14th–13th century BC with distinctive facial features were discovered in a Canaanite cemetery near Deir el-Balah, south of Gaza. Although reminiscent in shape of Egyptian mummy cases, the coffins are made of local clay. Offerings found near and around them are also shown: they include alabaster and bronze vessels, figurines, jewelry made of carnelian and gold, and pottery from Egypt and Mycenaean Greece. The fact that many of these items were imported sheds light on the regional trade of the time.

The Israelite period, which accounts for the largest group of items in the Hecht Museum, is represented by pottery vessels as well as a collection of fertility figurines. Additional vessels, coins, glass, figurines, seals, weights, and many other items illustrate life in the country during the Hellenistic, Roman, and Byzantine periods. A favorite is a bronze bread stamp depicting a menorah and inscribed in Greek "Belonging to Isaac."

A visit to the Hecht Museum offers the bonus of an opportunity to observe life at one of the country's leading universities.

ISRAEL EDIBLE OIL MUSEUM
Shemen Old Factory Compound
Haifa

HOURS: Sun.–Thurs. 9–12

TEL.: 04–670491
ADMISSION: Free

Focus: Ancient and Modern Oil Production

Courtyard with oil press

The production of oil (Heb. *shemen*)—vegetable oils but more especially olive oil—has been an important industry in the country for over 5,000 years. Its entire history—ancient methods of oil production, the development of oil technology, and the processing systems currently employed in the oil industry—is covered in this museum, located within the compound of the Shemen Factory in Haifa.

In the spacious courtyard of the Shemen Factory compound two reconstructed oil presses have been set up. One is a lever-and-screw press from the Byzantine era; the other, though built in the early 20th century, crushes olives between two flat grinding stones, a method used since biblical times. Nearby is a selection of stone weights, crushers, and lever weights. During the olive harvest, visitors are invited to try their hand at working these reconstructed oil presses.

On the main floor are exhibits devoted to oil production and its uses in the biblical period. Among the highlights is an installation for oil manufacturing dating from the 8th or 7th century BC, and a selection of ancient oil lamps. The contemporary oil industry and its by-products are depicted in exhibits on the second floor.

Future plans for this museum include the installation of additional participatory exhibits and the establishment of a library and archives with cassettes, slides, and audiovisual materials relating to ancient and modern oil production.

ISRAEL STATE RAILWAY MUSEUM

Old Haifa East Railway Station
Kikar Faisal
Haifa

HOURS: Sun., Tues., Thurs. 10–13

TEL.: 04–564293
ADMISSION: Free

Focus: **History of Local Railways**

This museum, housed in a group of stone buildings from the Ottoman period (one of which was the Haifa East Railway Station), provides visitors with a glimpse of Middle Eastern train travel in the brief era when it was possible to go by rail from Haifa direct to Beirut; to Cairo, via Kantara on the Sinai Peninsula; and to Amman or Damascus via the Valley Line. The rolling stock exhibited here includes two diesel locomotives, three cabooses, and five passenger and cargo cars. Among the oldest is an 1893 coach brought from Egypt and used as an ambulance in World War I; the most elegant is a "Royal Coach," a 1922 British-made wood-paneled car used for the transportation of visiting dignitaries.

Preserved here, in addition to documents, stamps, photographs, timetables, tickets, and other artifacts connected with local railways since their inception in the 1880s, are the quaint old machine that printed the train tickets and the bell that announced the departure of trains—which were notoriously late.

Labels are in Hebrew only, but visitors generally find that English translations are not essential. In this hands-on museum, climbing into and exploring the antique railroad cars is the main activity.

MANÉ-KATZ MUSEUM

89 Yefe Nof Street
Mount Carmel
Haifa

HOURS: Sun.–Thurs. 10–13 and 16–18, Sat. 10–13   TEL.: 04–383482
(subject to change in winter)   ADMISSION: Free

Focus: **Paintings by Mané-Katz and His Judaica Collection**

Situated just below the crest of Mount Carmel, with a panoramic view of the bay, is the whitewashed stucco house where painter Mané-Katz (Emmanuel Katz) spent his last years.

Born in the Ukraine in 1894, Mané-Katz joined the circle of artists who lived and worked in Paris between the two world wars. Color, more than form or composition, was Mané-Katz's dominant means of expression. Toward the end of his life he wrote, "Details are less important than the spirit of the work, the atmosphere, the feelings."

On view in this small museum on a rotating basis are works chosen from

Horses *by*
Mané-Katz

Wedding *by*
Mané-Katz

the several hundred oil paintings, drawings, and sculptures that the artist bequeathed to the city of Haifa at his death, in 1962. Also exhibited are selections from his collection of Judaica and objets d'art. This turn-of-the-century house and studio, furnished with antiques and Persian rugs, affords an interesting glimpse into the life and work of an important 20th-century Jewish artist.

THE MUSEUM OF JAPANESE ART/ TIKOTIN MUSEUM

89 Hanassi Avenue
Mount Carmel
Haifa

HOURS: Sun.–Thurs. 10–17, Sat. 10–14

TEL.: 04–383554
ADMISSION: $1.50

Focus: **18th–20th-Century Japanese Prints; Applied Arts**

This museum, located on the summit of Mount Carmel, was established in 1957 by Felix Tikotin, a Dutch Jewish antiques dealer. Devoted to the art of Japan, it adheres to the Japanese tradition of displaying beautiful objects that are in harmony with the season; exhibits therefore change frequently. In these galleries, shoji—sliding doors and partitions made of wood and paper—soften the harsh sunlight. In the distinctly Japanese atmosphere thus created are

Woman with Servant
*by Utamaro,
18th-century
hanging scroll,
watercolor on silk*

displayed screens, scrolls, pottery and porcelain, netsuke and inro, lacquer and metalwork, paintings from several schools, modern prints, and a variety of fresh flower arrangements.

The famous 17th–19th-century ukiyo-e prints of Edo (as Tokyo was formerly known), depicting scenes of the "floating world"—a world of pleasure in which Kabuki actors and geisha are conspicuous—are well represented. The collection includes prints by Harunobu, Hiroshige, Hokusai, and Kuniyoshi, and even a rare drawing attributed to the elusive Sharaku.

The museum has an extensive reference library comprising approximately 2,500 books on the art and culture of Japan. Arrangements to use the library should be made in advance.

NATIONAL MARITIME MUSEUM

198 Allenby Road
Haifa

HOURS: Sun.–Thurs. 10–16, Sat. 10–13

TEL.: 04–536622
ADMISSION: $2.50

Focus: **History of Shipping; Underwater Archaeology**

Model of Egyptian funerary boat

Wood figurine of a swimmer, Egyptian, 15th century BC

Occupying a modern four-story building located near the entrance to Haifa from the south, this museum, founded by Arie Ben Eli, chronicles over 5,000 years of maritime history, with emphasis on the Eastern Mediterranean, cradle of shipping in the Western world.

In spacious, well-lighted galleries the sea and seafaring, from ancient times to the present, take center stage. Detailed models illustrate the development of maritime technology, along with reproductions of ancient ships built according to representations in ancient wall paintings and reliefs, models of famous ships throughout history, and such examples of modern nautical architecture as a model of an oil rig on the North Sea. There is an extensive collection of coins bearing maritime motifs, and one of navigational charts and maps published since the 15th century (few earlier examples have survived). Among the many navigational instruments is a handsome 10th-century Chinese astronomical device carved in jade.

The National Maritime Museum features a rich collection of archaeological artifacts. The earliest are ancient Egyptian funerary boats, made of wood,

Entrance with cannon

and terra-cotta cultic boats from Cyprus, dating from the 2nd millennium BC. Clay models of boats found in Hellenistic and Roman tombs are complete with anchors and fishing equipment. Numerous statues of creatures of the deep—monsters, gods, and fish—as well as many paintings, drawings, and prints, show the power that the sea has exercised over the imagination of man since ancient times.

Underwater archaeology is another subject highlighted here. Some of the exciting finds that have been made within a few miles of this museum include Egyptian stone anchors, Greek amphorae, Roman weapons, and Islamic coins retrieved from various ancient wrecks. In addition to these artifacts, dioramas and photomurals enhance the presentation of current underwater archaeological work in Israel and help explain the new techniques. Outstanding among the treasures that the sea has yielded is a bronze ram from a 4th- or 3rd-

Bronze ram from warship, c. 400 BC

century BC battleship, found off the coast near Atlit; it is strikingly decorated with the trident of the sea god Poseidon and other motifs.

The museum's program includes lectures and seminars, and research and restoration work are conducted in its laboratories. A library of some 5,000 volumes dealing with the history of seafaring and with underwater archaeology is open to students and researchers by appointment.

TECHNODA/NATIONAL MUSEUM OF SCIENCE AND TECHNOLOGY
Balfour Street (opposite #15)
Old Technion Campus
Haifa

HOURS: Mon.–Thurs. 9–17 (Tues. to 19), Fri. 9–13, Sat. 10–14	TEL.: 04–671372 ADMISSION: $2.00

Focus: **Explaining Science through Participatory Exhibits**

Technoda, one of Israel's largest science museums, was founded by Professors Zvi Dori and Yitzhak Oref of the Chemistry Department of Technion, in the belief that direct demonstrations and participatory exhibits best enable lay people to gain an understanding of natural phenomena and scientific laws. The museum occupies part of the building that formerly housed Technion, the first institute of higher learning in the country, established in 1924. The structure itself is noteworthy: designed by Alexander Bearwald, it was an early venture in combining modern and Middle Eastern architectural styles.

At Technoda the visitor is the prime mover: the principles of physics, chemistry, mathematics, and mechanics are brought to life by turning a knob or pushing a button. Among the scientific phenomena explored here are lasers, solar energy, optics, acoustics, and photochemistry. Exhibits that illustrate the practical application of scientific laws include a wind tunnel, a miniature solar-powered train, an artillery computer, and a model of an air-to-air missile.

Technoda features attractive, colorful displays, extensive text panels, and clear instructions in both English and Hebrew. Its popularity with high school students proves how effective this museum has been—so much so that the present facilities are sometimes strained to their limits. Current plans call for an eventual expansion into the rest of the former Technion building.

GALILEE

ACRE MUNICIPAL MUSEUM
Old City
Acre

HOURS: Sun.–Thurs. 9–17, Fri. and Sat. 9–14   TEL.: 04–918251 (ext. 343)
                                                    ADMISSION: Free

Focus: 4,000 Years of Acre's History

Acre's long history is recalled in this museum, located in the heart of the Old City in a structure still known in Arabic as Hammam el-Pasha (Bathhouse of the Pasha"). It was built at the end of the 18th century by Pasha Ahmad el-Jazzar ("the Butcher"), the Ottoman governor of the region, who is remembered in European annals for his role in withstanding Napoleon's siege of Acre in 1799. The bathhouse building—with its marble floors, glazed wall tiles, and large domed hall, where light filters in through small, multicolored glass panes in the vault—evokes vivid images of the Ottoman period.

The varied exhibits here include artifacts from many periods of Acre's 4,000-year existence. One of the country's most important harbor cities, Acre is referred to in the Bible (Acco; Judges 1:31) and in ancient Egyptian and Mesopotamian records. During the Hellenistic period it was renamed Ptolemais, in honor of Ptolemy I, king of Egypt, and it was visited by the apostle Paul during his travels in the 1st century. More than a millennium later it was captured by the Crusaders, and as Saint-Jean-d'Acre it became their capital after the fall of Jerusalem in 1187. The loss of Acre to the Mamluks in 1291 marked the end of the Crusader kingdom in the Holy Land.

Among the objects exhibited are pottery, statuary, and weapons excavated in Acre and the immediate vicinity. Also displayed are a collection of Roman glass, glazed Persian ceramics of the 9th century, and a selection of Crusader sculptures and inscriptions carved in stone. Enlarged maps show the city's development under successive rulers and detail the events of the Napoleonic siege. A separate room is devoted to Arab folklore and folkways, with examples of traditional costumes and jewelry.

The exhibits here would benefit from more extensive labeling; few dates are provided, and the historical background is minimal. Yet the well-preserved Ottoman *hammam* is itself a landmark well worth visiting during a tour of Acre. (The *hammam* is located next to the Halls of the Hospitallers.)

YIGAL ALLON CENTER

Kibbutz Ginnosar

HOURS: Sun.–Thurs. 9–15, Fri. 9–13, Sat. 9–15
Refreshments available at kibbutz guest house

TEL.: 06–721495
ADMISSION: $2.50

Focus: **Settlement in Galilee—Archaeology, History, Ethnography**

Yigal Allon Center on the Sea of Galilee

The Yigal Allon Center provides an excellent introduction to the history and ecology of Galilee. An educational enterprise whose theme is "Man in the Galilee," it is a fitting memorial to Yigal Allon (1918–1980), a native of Galilee, a founding member of Kibbutz Ginnosar, a builder of Israel's army, and a national leader deeply concerned with issues of peace.

This impressive circular building on the shore of the Sea of Galilee—its interior furbished with olive wood and basalt—is an appropriate setting for a display of paintings and photographs depicting the beauty of the region. Here, too, groups of lifelike figures portray some of the characteristic lifestyles of the area in successive periods since antiquity. Other exhibits include a model of a Jewish town showing daily life during the time of the Mishna and Talmud, and a re-creation of a contemporary Arab village, where a traditional way of life encounters modernity. A manually operated "clock" demonstrates the development of human settlement in Galilee; each century is represented by a different view.

A remarkable discovery, made in 1986 during a dramatic drop in the level of the Sea of Galilee, is a 27-foot wooden boat. Now immersed in a special preservative solution, with fish from the Sea of Galilee swimming around it, the boat appears to date from the period of the 1st century BC and the 1st century AD. The find aroused great interest because of a possible connection with the fishermen of the small Jewish communities that flourished here during the time of the early ministry of Jesus. It is plausible that the boat was lost during a fierce battle that took place here in AD 67 between the Jews of Migdal and the soldiers of Vespasian, ending in a crushing defeat of the Jews, whose boats were sunk by the Romans until "the sea was red as blood" (Josephus, *The Jewish War* 3:526).

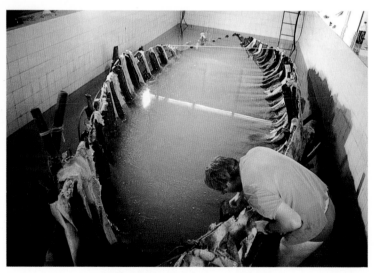

2,000-year-old boat found in the Sea of Galilee

BAR DAVID INSTITUTE OF JEWISH ART

Kibbutz Bar'am

HOURS: Sun., Tues., Thurs. 8–13, Sat. 10–11 and 12–14

TEL.: 06–988295
ADMISSION: Free

Focus: Archaeology; Judaica; Israeli Art

Remains of Bar'am synagogue, 3rd century

Despite their geographical isolation on Israel's northern border, the dedicated members of Kibbutz Bar'am have been able to maintain not only a museum but also an active year-round program of exhibits, lectures, and classes on archaeology and Jewish art geared to the interests of the schoolchildren of the area. All programs are coordinated with local schools.

Exhibits, which change every six weeks, utilize the museum's own collections; from time to time special traveling exhibits from the Israel Museum are featured. On permanent exhibition is an excellent, if limited, collection of archaeological artifacts, including glass vessels, Luristan bronzes, and a group of oil lamps. From more recent times, but by an unknown artist, comes a series of 18th-century paintings on glass depicting the biblical story of Joseph. The museum's well-displayed Judaica collection contains, among the ritual objects, an interesting Hanukkah lamp from Salonika.

The museum also owns approximately 600 works by contemporary Israeli painters and sculptors, and it regularly mounts exhibits drawn from this collection. As part of its cultural enrichment program, the kibbutz periodically invites artists to live and work at Bar'am.

Close by, and well worth the short drive, are the impressive remains of the 3rd-century Bar'am synagogue. This elevated site affords a view of northern Galilee.

BEIT GORDON
Kibbutz Deganya Alef

HOURS: Sun.–Thurs. 9–16, Fri. 9–12, Sat. 9–12　　　　TEL.: 06–750040
ADMISSION: $2.50

Focus: **Regional Settlement from Prehistoric Times to the Present; Flora, Fauna, and Minerals**

Beit Gordon—comprising an observatory, a lecture hall, a library, and a museum—is named for Aaron David Gordon (1856–1922), a pioneering leader of the Zionist movement and a passionate advocate of the return of the Jews to tilling the soil. It is located on the grounds of Kibbutz Deganya—established in 1911 and known as *em hakvutzot* ("mother of the collective settlements")— where Gordon spent the last years of his life.

In the natural history section of the museum, exhibits illustrate the geology, zoology, and botany of the area. Examples of indigenous mammals, birds, reptiles, fish, insects, plants, flowers, fossils, and minerals form the nucleus of a comprehensive and well-presented collection. Special emphasis is

placed on the ecology of the Jordan Valley and the area of Lake Kinneret (the Sea of Galilee).

A relatively new section of Beit Gordon is devoted to the history of human settlement in the area; the displays begin with prehistoric artifacts dating from approximately 1,000,000 years ago. Representative archaeological finds illustrate the rise of agriculture in the Neolithic period and the patterns of the later cultures of the country. Special thematic exhibits center on the develop-

ment of the alphabet and the techniques of fishing and sailing over the past 5,000 years. Outside the museum, both ancient and modern agricultural implements are on view.

"If you ignore nature you ignore yourself," wrote Gordon. This museum is a fitting monument to the man who did so much to awaken a positive attitude toward nature and to spread the concept of the dignity of labor in the Jewish community of Palestine. A section of the museum's library is devoted to Gordon's works, including the many translations of his books.

BEIT HAMEIRI
Old City, Safed

HOURS: Sun.–Thurs. 9–14, Fri. 9–1   TEL.: 06–971307
ADMISSION: $1.50

> *Focus:* **Life in Safed at the Turn of the Century**

The group of small houses now known as Beit Hameiri were built in 1517 and have survived the many earthquakes, civil disturbances, and wars that Safed has faced over the centuries. In 1959, Yehezkiel Hameiri, a member of a prominent Safed family that had lived in the city for five generations, transformed the complex into a museum and educational center devoted to the history and culture of the Jewish community of Safed.

Located in the mountains of Upper Galilee, Safed became prominent during the Crusader period, when it was the site of a huge fortress. Under the Mamluks, it served as the capital of the northern district of Palestine. Jews first came to Safed in large numbers at the end of the 15th century, after their expulsion from Spain; by the 16th century Safed had become one of the most important Jewish spiritual centers in the world. Under the leadership of such famous scholars as rabbis Itzhak Lurie and Yoseph Caro, the mystical tradition of Kabbalah flourished and the city became a center of learning. The first printing press in the country was established here in 1563, and the first Hebrew book, *Lekah Tov (Good Lesson)*, written by one of Caro's disciples, was printed in Safed in 1578.

Beit Hameiri chronicles the life of the Jewish community in Safed, with special emphasis on the late 19th and early 20th century. Exhibits include kitchen utensils, furniture, antique clothing, lamps, and tools and machinery. The museum's historical section contains photographs, documents, and memorabilia that reflect the impact of events such as the great earthquake of 1837, the Arab riots in 1936–38, and Israel's War of Independence, in 1948.

Negotiating the steep, winding alleys of the Old City to find Beit Hameiri may present a challenge, but it also offers an opportunity to discover many other points of interest. The Old City's galleries, cafés, elaborate synagogues, and artists' studios are certainly worth exploring on foot, especially in summer (in the cold winter months places tend to close).

BEIT HASHOMER
Kfar Giladi

HOURS: Sun.–Thurs. 8–12 and 14–16, Fri. and Sat. 8:30–12   TEL.: 06–941565
ADMISSION: $1.00

Focus: **History of Hashomer ("The Watchman")**

The personalities and events connected with Hashomer, an early Jewish defense organization, are commemorated in this museum. Kfar Giladi, the kibbutz where it is located, was founded in 1916 by 20 members of Hashomer who originally came from Russia and Poland. Their leader, Israel Giladi, chose this site in Upper Galilee to further the organization's main goals: expanding the area of Jewish settlement in Palestine and protecting the lives and property of its inhabitants.

As the exhibits here reveal, organized self-defense by Jews commenced in Jerusalem in the late 19th century. The beginnings of Hashomer can be placed in 1907, when a group of young Zionist workers in Jaffa founded a watchmen's society named Bar Giora (after one of the last defenders of Jerusalem in the struggle against the Romans in the 1st century AD). Two years later, in 1909, Hashomer was officially established to protect Jewish farmers and settlers from harassment and attacks by Beduin and hostile Arab villagers. The members of Hashomer, who patrolled on horseback and carried rifles, typified the emerging Zionist ideal of the self-reliant settler.

Effectively displayed documents, letters, maps, and photographs illustrate the history of the Hashomer organization and its role in the development of modern Jewish settlements in the region. A slide show, in Hebrew and English, provides additional historical background.

BEIT LOHAMEI HAGHETAOT

Kibbutz Lohamei Haghetaot

HOURS: Sun.–Thurs. 9–16, Fri. 9–13, Sat. 10–17
Refreshments available at kiosk

TEL.: 04–920412
ADMISSION: Free

Focus: The Holocaust and the Resistance

Beit Lohamei Haghetaot

Created to convey in graphic terms the story of the Holocaust and of the Jewish resistance during World War II, this museum is named for "the fighters of the ghettos" (Heb. *lohamei haghetaot*). Pictures, maps, documents, and models portray the life and culture of the Jewish communities of Europe before their destruction, the fate of those in the ghettos and the concentration camps, the spiritual resistance and the armed revolt, and partisan and underground activity in every country under German occupation.

Skillfully set up on the ground floor is an exhibit devoted to Jewish life in both the cities and the small towns of Poland and Lithuania during the early years of this century, including detailed models of the ghettos of Warsaw and Vilna. On the second floor, photomurals and text panels trace the rise of Nazism and its expansion throughout Europe. A replica of Anne Frank's

Model of Vilna ghetto

house in Amsterdam is to be seen here. Also exhibited is the glass booth in which Adolph Eichmann stood trial in Jerusalem in 1960.

In one of the exhibits, the history of Hungarian Jewry during the Holocaust can be followed. Two galleries are devoted to Holocaust art; among the works are drawings by the children of Theresienstadt. Chronicled here too is the work of the poet Yitzhak Katznelson, who perished in Auschwitz and to whose memory the museum is dedicated.

Beit Lohamei Haghetaot, in its coverage of these dark years, performs a valuable service, especially for young people: it brings into focus aspects of the Holocaust not normally dealt with in history textbooks. Its exhibits offer glimpses of the culture and traditions of Jewish communities in pre–World War II Europe that no longer exist. The Beit Lohamei Haghetaot complex includes, in addition to the museum, a repository of Holocaust documents, a library, and a film archive.

BEIT USSISHKIN

Kibbutz Dan

HOURS: Sun.–Thurs. 9–15, Fri. 9–12, Sat. 10–14   TEL: 06–941704
ADMISSION: $.75

> *Focus:* **Natural History and Archaeology of the Hula Valley Region**

The low-lying stone building that houses this natural history museum faces snowcapped Mount Hermon and blends into the dramatic landscape; it was designed by architect Leopold Krakauer. Opened in 1955, the museum, named after Zionist leader Menachem Ussishkin (1863–1941), is devoted to the preservation of both historical artifacts and specimens of the regional flora and fauna. Since the Hula marshes have now been drained and transformed into rich farmland, many of the plants and birds once indigenous to the unique wetlands habitat can now be seen only at Beit Ussishkin. The area is also of great geological interest, since the Hula basin is surrounded by the Golan, Mount Hermon, and the Naphtali Mountains, some of which rise to 10,000 feet above sea level. As for archaeological material, the excavations of the biblical city of Dan, just a few miles north of the kibbutz, have supplied the museum with a wealth of finds.

The exhibits at Beit Ussishkin are divided into several sections. One deals with the Hula basin and the history of human habitation in the area, which began in the Stone Age. It includes ancient stone tools, clay vessels, models of Canaanite and Israelite city gates and fortification walls, and inscriptions uncovered in the excavations of Tel Dan. The story of Jewish resettlement in the Hula basin in the 20th century is also documented. In the natural history section, dioramas combine general information on the topics of biology and zoology with mounted specimens of mammals, insects, reptiles, fish, and birds native to this area. From Mount Hermon and the Golan Heights come a variety of animal species that cannot be seen elsewhere.

Like many regional museums in Israel, Beit Ussishkin conducts a wide-ranging educational program for local schools. The museum also has a library that is available to scholars and a good selection of short films about the region and its water resources.

Visitors should take the opportunity of touring the nearby Tel Dan excavations, which are situated in a verdant nature reserve near one of the main sources of the Jordan River. Among the highlights of the site is a well-preserved city gate from the Middle Bronze Age, when the city (known as Laish) was an important Canaanite center. Other impressive structures date from the Iron Age, when Dan became a place of religious pilgrimage for the people of the northern kingdom of Israel. Aside from its archaeological importance, Dan is worth visiting for its spectacular scenery: the Hula Valley, the Golan Heights, and Mount Hermon.

*Tel Dan
excavations*

DUBROVIN FARM MUSEUM

Yesud Hama'ala

HOURS: Sun.–Thurs. 8–17, Fri. 8–14, Sat. 8–17   TEL.: 06–937371
Café and bar in the reconstructed stables   ADMISSION: $1.50

Focus: **History of the Settlement; Story of the Dubrovin family**

Among the orchards surrounding the settlement of Yesud Hama'ala is a group of restored stone buildings with red-tile roofs that house exhibits depicting the early history of the settlement and the daily life of the Dubrovin family. The biblical phrase *yesud hama'ala* (began to go up), which the settlement adopted as its name, is from the passage in the Book of Ezra (7:9) describing the sage's return to Jerusalem from exile in Babylon.

The settlement was established in 1884, on land purchased by a group of Jewish immigrants from Russia, members of the Hovevei Zion (Lovers of Zion), who intended to settle and farm there. The land, located in the rich Hula Valley, looked lush, and water was plentiful. Unfortunately the deceptively green countryside was on the edge of malarial swamps, and many of the settlers and their children died here in the first decades, before it became standard practice to take daily doses of quinine. In time, the settlers drained the surrounding swamps, planted fruit orchards, and even experimented with

Dubrovin Farm Museum

raising flowers for the production of perfume. Wheat, apples, plums, and pecans are currently the settlement's main crops.

The Dubrovin Farm Museum tells a story that began in Russia at the end of the 19th century with Andrei Dubrovin, a Russian peasant who became a Subbotnik—a Christian Sabbatarian (observer of Saturday as the Sabbath). Harassed by the Russian Orthodox clergy, Andrei eventually converted to Judaism; he changed his name to Yoav and decided to make his home in the land of the Bible. Together with his wife and their eight children, he immigrated to Palestine; he bought land and settled in Yesud Hama'ala in 1904. Like his neighbors, he suffered from malaria, and he lost two sons and several grandchildren to the disease. Because of his size and his courage, Andrei Dubrovin is remembered as the "Galilean Goliath," a heroic figure who taught Jewish settlers how to till the land.

After the last of the descendants of the Dubrovin family died, at the age of ninety-five, several government agencies and private individuals joined together to purchase the farm and turn it into a museum, and the Dubrovin house, stables, dairy, and workshops have been restored to their appearance in the early 20th century. Note should be taken of the cistern in the courtyard, where water was drawn by a series of buckets, utilizing donkey or mule power.

A personal tour of Yesud Hama'ala is offered by Arik Lubosky, a descendant of one of the early settlers; he can be reached by telephone or by mail at Yesud Hama'ala, Upper Galilee 12105.

EIN DOR MUSEUM OF ARCHAEOLOGY
Kibbutz Ein Dor

HOURS: By appointment	TEL.: 06–768111 or 06–768333
	ADMISSION: Free

Focus: **Regional Archaeology; Memorial to the Fallen Soldiers of the Kibbutz**

This new archaeological museum forms part of a cultural center for the residents of the area. Kibbutz Ein Dor lies in the shadow of Mount Tabor, surrounded by attractive garden homes and green fields. In biblical times the site was the home of the "witch of Endor," whose occult services were sought by King Saul shortly before his battle with the Philistines (1 Samuel 28:7).

Courtyard with oil presses

Outside the museum are several restored oil presses, which visitors are encouraged to try their hand at operating. Inside, in the main exhibition gallery, are assemblages of ancient stone tools, domestic pottery, and coins, grouped chronologically. A special display, including mosaics from a nearby synagogue at Kfar Matzar, features finds from the time of the compilation of the Mishna—the Late Roman period.

A special room in the museum, called Yad Lebanim (Memorial to the Sons), is dedicated to members of the kibbutz who fell in Israel's wars.

This small, well-designed museum offers both adults and children a real learning experience. Its clearly presented exhibits do not require any prior knowledge of the archaeology of the country or of this area in particular.

Yad Lebanim (Memorial to the Sons)

GOLAN ARCHAEOLOGICAL MUSEUM
Katzrin

HOURS: Sun.–Thurs. 9–16, Fri. 9–13, Sat. 10–13   TEL.: 06–961350
Café nearby   ADMISSION: $1.50

Focus: **Archaeological Discoveries from Gamla, Katzrin, and Other Sites on the Golan**

The Golan Archaeological Museum occupies a modern structure built of concrete, glass, and local basalt. Its collections, while not extensive, effectively trace the history of human settlement in the Golan from prehistoric times to the end of the Byzantine period, in the 7th century.

The earliest of the finds exhibited here are flint and basalt tools and fossilized animal bones (500,000–5000 BC). Agriculture in the area began in the fourth millennium BC, in the Chalcolithic period. The remains of a house of that period, reassembled inside the museum, contain various domestic objects found in the house, among them large clay storage jars, basalt grinding mills, and a pillar-form stone statue with facial features—a domestic cult ob-

Basalt relief with menorah, shofar, and incense shovel, 5th century

Opposite: Remains of 4th-millennium BC house with storage jars

ject unique to the Golan. The display is enhanced by a photomural of the house in situ. Also found on the Golan is the dolmen, or megalithic tomb structure built of large, roughly dressed stone slabs; an example is shown here beside an assemblage of pottery and weapons from the Bronze Age.

The museum features a striking display devoted to Gamla, a nearby site, where the Jews fought valiantly against Vespasian in AD 67, during the First Revolt; a detailed model of the ancient fortress is shown, as well as selected finds from excavations conducted at the site, among them arrowheads, ballista stones, clay oil lamps, and coins.

In the museum's courtyard can be seen an impressive array of architectural elements from synagogues and churches on the Golan. They are some of the extensive remains from the Byzantine period, which indicate an increasing density of population in the area. With the destruction of Jerusalem and the Temple in AD 70, the center of Jewish life gradually moved north, and many Jews settled on the Golan. (To date, 27 sites have been discovered.) At the museum are dozens of lintels, beams, columns, pillars, and capitals from synagogues and churches, as well as tombstones and sarcophagi, made of basalt and highly decorated in relief with animal, plant, and geometric motifs. Some remains bear inscriptions in Hebrew or Aramaic, silent testimony to a rich and diverse past.

Many of the artifacts at the museum come from the two sites of Gamla and Katzrin, which are well worth visiting. The scenery at Gamla is spectacular: waterfalls rush down the valleys below and the Sea of Galilee glistens in the distance. Occasionally, vultures with their seven-foot wingspread hover

Remains of 5th-century synagogue

overhead. The city, in the words of Josephus, "was situated upon a rough ridge of a high mountain, with a kind of sinew in the middle . . . insomuch that it is like a camel [*gamla* in Aramaic] in figure, from whence it is so named" (*The Jewish War* 4:1:1). According to the historian, in AD 67, after 4,000 Jewish warriors had fallen before the Roman troops, 5,000 others, realizing that the battle was lost, flung themselves from the narrow ridge into the valley. Within the ruins of the fortified city are the remains of one of the earliest synagogues yet found in the land, destroyed when Gamla fell. The best-preserved synagogue on the Golan is in the village of Katzrin. The site has been designated Ancient Katzrin Park. Excavations began in 1979, and the synagogue and several houses of the Talmudic-period village have been partially restored. The synagogue, which dates from the 5th century and which stands on the remains of an earlier one, was destroyed in a major earthquake in 746, when the village was abandoned. It was built of dressed basalt blocks and was divided by two rows of columns into a nave and two aisles. The platform on which the Torah shrine stood is oriented toward Jerusalem, in the south. (For more details about the "Talmudic Village and Synagogue" in Ancient Katzrin Park, call 06–962412.)

GOLANI BRIGADE MUSEUM AND COMMEMORATION SITE

Golani Junction

HOURS: Sun.–Thurs. 9–16, Fri. 9–13, Sat. 9–17   TEL.: 06-767215
Refreshments available at kiosk on premises   ADMISSION: $1.50

Focus: **History of the Golani Brigade**

On the summit of a hill commanding a spectacular view of Lower Galilee, the city of Tiberias, and the Sea of Galilee stand this museum and monument, established as a memorial to the fallen soldiers of the Golani Brigade, an elite unit of the Israel Defense Forces; they commemorate the courage, heroism, and dedication shown in the brigade's many battles "fought all over the Land of Israel, in Galilee, and in the Negev, in the Sinai and in the Golan Heights, on the northern border and in southern Lebanon." Designed by architect Yosef Assa, the unusual structure of exposed concrete resembles a series of bunkers.

The museum itself consists of three of the bunker-like units, whose dark, closed-in atmosphere conveys a sense of being in the front line of battle. In the first exhibition hall, the theme is the tradition of the Israel Defense Forces epitomized by the slogan "Follow me!"—the tradition of commanders leading their troops into battle as did Barak and Gideon in the days of the Judges. Exhibits in the second hall, where the theme is "On the Battlefield," feature maps, battle plans, photographs, reliefs, and documents, as well as weapons and personal memorabilia.

An underground tunnel leads into a dimly lighted memorial hall named Yizkor (Remembrance). Here the records of over 1,000 fallen soldiers of the Golani Brigade are housed, each volume bound in white jute cloth with the name and serial number of the soldier on the cover. The memorial hall, like the commemoration site of which it is a part, testifies eloquently to the high cost of war.

HANITA MUSEUM
Kibbutz Hanita

HOURS: Sun.–Fri. 8–12, Sat. by appointment   TEL.: 04–859677
ADMISSION: $1.00

Focus: **Hanita in Ancient and Modern Times**

Hanita, a place mentioned in the Talmud, has since antiquity guarded the passes leading from the mountains of Lebanon to the fertile valleys of western Galilee and the coastal cities of Achziv and Acre; its long history comes to life in this museum.

Flora and fauna typical of the region are on display in the museum's entrance hall. The archaeological collection includes artifacts from many periods of Hanita's history: stone tools from the Chalcolithic period, a Phoenician inscription, coins issued in the nearby city of Tyre, mosaics with intricate designs from a 5th-century Byzantine church, and decorated ceramic vessels from the Early Arab and Crusader periods.

Two rooms are devoted to the modern history of Kibbutz Hanita, which was founded in 1938 as one of the *homa u'migdal* ("tower and stockade") settlements built throughout the country in the late 1930s in an attempt to expand the area owned by Jews. Hanita was established in a single day with the help of 140 volunteers, who carried building materials, tools, arms, and supplies to the site. Of the 90 settlers who remained at Hanita—in tents behind a barbed-wire fence—2 were killed on the first night. This section of the museum features photographs and documents, models of other tower and stockade settlements, and an unusual communications device that transmitted Morse code messages through reflecting mirrors catching the sun.

The story of Hanita's continuing struggle is brought up to date with a display of some of the Katyusha shells fired from southern Lebanon that fell on Hanita in 1983.

HAZOR MUSEUM
Kibbutz Ayelet Hashahar

HOURS: Sun.–Thurs. 8–16, Fri. 8–15
Refreshments available at kibbutz guest house

TEL.: 06–934855
ADMISSION: $1.50

Focus: **Archaeological Finds from Tel Hazor**

This small museum, designed by David Reznik and Nahum Maron and opened to the public in 1966, makes for a pleasant stop after a visit to nearby Hazor, one of the most important archaeological sites in the country. First extensively excavated in the 1950s by Yigael Yadin on behalf of the Israel Exploration Fund and the Hebrew University, ancient Hazor covered an area of nearly 2,000 acres and dominated a major junction of overland trade routes.

During the Bronze Age, Hazor was one of the largest cities in the region and was in commercial contact with Egypt, Anatolia, and Mesopotamia. Hammurabi's ambassador resided in Canaanite Hazor. Its reputation as "head of all those kingdoms" (Joshua 11:10) ended with its complete destruction, presumably by the invading Israelites, at the end of the Late Bronze Age. Although rebuilt by the Israelites, Hazor never regained its former commercial and political importance as a regional center. Solomon, and later Omri, fortified the city; remains of a six-chambered Solomonic gate and case-

Lion orthostat, Orthostat Temple, Hazor

mate wall can still be seen in the excavations on the acropolis, or upper fortified part of the city.

At the entrance to the Hazor Museum is a large-scale cross section of the upper and lower areas of Hazor, showing the 21 superimposed levels of occupation. Finds of pottery vessels, bronze and stone figurines, and jewelry, arranged chronologically, illustrate the main cultural influences on Hazor.

Opposite: Excavations at Tel Hazor with snow-capped Mount Hermon in background

Highlights here are models of two of the Late Bronze Age Canaanite temples excavated in Hazor and an actual-size replica of the famous Shrine of the Stelae now in the Israel Museum (see page 33), a group of basalt ritual images—ten stelae (one carved with two hands raised toward a crescent moon), a seated male figure, an offering table, and a lion orthostat.

The displays here, well labeled in both English and Hebrew, testify to the importance of the ancient city of Hazor.

HULA NATURE RESERVE AND VISITORS CENTER

Yesud Hama'ala

HOURS: Daily: summer 8–16, winter 8–15   TEL.: 06–961350 or 06–962412
Shaded picnic area and snack bar at the site   ADMISSION: $1.00

Focus: **Regional Ecology**

Founded in 1956, this was the first of Israel's 120 nature reserves. It is located among the agricultural fields and fish ponds that occupy the area of the formerly malarial Hula swamps. The bird life of the Hula reserve is especially interesting, since migrating birds come here from as far away as Russia and Scandinavia on their way to wintering grounds in Africa.

A 14-minute slide show in both English and Hebrew gives an introduction to the natural history of the site. The museum features an excellent model of the local water resources, showing how the Hula swamps were drained and illustrating the area's ecology. Displays of the indigenous flowers of the Hula marshes highlight the white water lily (*Nymphaea alba*) and the yellow pond lily (*Nuphar luteum*). The reserve's 200 acres of papyrus thickets are the habitat also for mollusks and crabs and provide nesting sites for herons, egrets, moorhens, and a variety of warblers. Exhibits currently in the planning stage will contain models of new agricultural systems and processes for fish production.

From a nature trail, occasionally interspersed with raised wooden walkways, it is possible to observe the indigenous flora and fauna, the most impressive of which are native water buffalo. The walk, just under a mile, takes approximately an hour and ends at an elevated observation tower. Guided tours are conducted every Saturday except for eight weeks in the fall.

HULA VALLEY REGIONAL MUSEUM
Kibbutz Ma'ayan Baruch

HOURS: Sun.–Fri. 9–12 TEL.: 06–944570 (ask for Amnon Assaf)
ADMISSION: $1.00

Focus: Prehistory of the Hula Valley

The Hula Valley Regional Museum is devoted to the subject of prehistoric human settlement in the area. Its collections also include finds from the historic periods, discovered around the kibbutz. An ethnographic exhibit features tools and craft productions from primitive societies all over the world.

Human skeleton as found in a burial

Paleolithic hand axes

At the entrance, visitors are introduced to the chronology of the prehistoric and historic periods by two large explanatory charts showing characteristic tools and pottery types of each era. Attractive wall murals depict reed rafts transporting papyrus across Lake Hula; other photographs show dolmens—megalithic tomb structures formed of rough stone slabs—and, from a much later period, a Crusader castle.

Display cases of artifacts proceed chronologically from the Lower Paleolithic period to the Natufian and Neolithic periods. Among the noteworthy Neolithic finds are whetstones, hammers, bone tools, stone bowls, flint scrapers, shell beads, sickle blades, and pottery. One section shows how the earliest stone tools were made; a nearby case exhibits 250,000-year-old elephant toes, teeth, and a tusk. A reconstructed burial of the Natufian period contains the bones of a baby with a necklace around its neck and body, an adult in the fetal position, and a puppy. (This may be the earliest example of the close connection between man and dog.) The collection of hand axes from the Paleolithic period—crude tools beautiful in their simplicity—is the special pride of Amnon Assaf, the museum's founder and director; it is the largest collection of its kind in the world.

The ethnographic section has been designed to demonstrate how people from all over the world have utilized local materials for the necessities of life. In some cultures the traditional shapes and designs of many tools, vessels, and garments have changed little over the millennia, so that even relatively recent examples shed light on the life of early humans. On display are a sheepskin coat and a turtle amulet, from the Golan; a loincloth made out of an ostrich egg, from Kenya; a robe made of palm branches stitched together, decorated with painted animals, from Peru; and a group of gourds, universally used for collecting and holding liquid, from the Golan, Kenya, Ethiopia, and South Africa.

Families, especially those with young children, are welcomed here. The museum has even provided a toy box filled with stuffed animals for children to play with while their parents linger at the exhibits in this inviting regional museum.

KFAR TAVOR HISTORICAL MUSEUM
Kfar Tavor

HOURS: Sun.–Thurs. 9–18, Fri. 9–12:30, Sat. 9–18   TEL.: 06–767583
ADMISSION: $1.00

Focus: History of the Settlement

The original schoolhouse of this settlement, which was established in 1901 on land purchased by Baron Edmond de Rothschild and was one of the first Jewish agricultural settlements in Lower Galilee, is its museum. Here are preserved thousands of documents, community records, photographs, and letters relating to the early history of Kfar Tavor and the activities of Hashomer (see Beit Hashomer, page 177).

Exhibits are divided into thematic sections dealing with 13 subjects, among them agriculture, religion, education, medicine, water and lighting, commerce, taxes, cooperative unions, law and order. On the balcony, or second level, of this 1903 building is a gallery featuring the paintings, based on biblical stories and themes, of Abraham Jaskiel.

Agricultural implements from the turn of the century are displayed on the grounds outside the museum. Nearby is a reconstruction of Kfar Tavor's first farm building.

LEHMANN MUSEUM AND
HAMMATH TIBERIAS SYNAGOGUE

Tiberias

HOURS: Sun.–Thurs. 8–16,
Fri. 9–13

For information call Tiberias Hot Springs
(across the road): 06–791967 or 06–791968
ADMISSION $1.00

Focus: **3rd–4th-Century Synagogue Mosaics**

One of the themes of this small, well-designed museum is the history of the hot baths of Tiberias, which still function as they did in antiquity. Also featured is the archaeological collection of Ernst Lehmann, founder of the museum.

In the foyer stands a replica of a large seven-branched stone candelabrum excavated in 1920 at the site of the 3rd–4th-century synagogue of Hammath Tiberias, a few steps away from the museum. Flowers and pomegranates are carved on the surface of the menorah, and each branch terminates in a small recess for oil. The original is in the Israel Museum.

Inside the museum, color-coordinated graphs and charts explain the geology of the area and analyze the mineral composition of the hot springs located throughout the area, which contain sulfur, chloride, magnesium, and other minerals and reach a temperature of approximately 140 degrees Fahrenheit. Their therapeutic properties have attracted attention as far back as Roman times.

Among the artifacts exhibited in the museum is pottery of the 1st century AD, the period during which the city of Tiberias was founded by Herod Antipas. The museum's exhibits also include a model of one of the thermal baths built in Tiberias in Ottoman times, and one of its details, a stone statue of a crouching lion, is evidence of the baths' continuous popularity: the original of the crouching lion can be seen at the edge of one of the large pools in the nearby bathhouse, which is still in use. According to tradition, a woman could be miraculously cured of barrenness by climbing onto this lion after bathing.

Outside the museum, visitors can proceed through a small park to the ruins of a 6th-century bathhouse. A short distance up the slope behind the museum are the remains of mosaic floors from the 4th-century synagogue of Hammath Tiberias, built when Tiberias was the spiritual capital of the Jewish community in Palestine. The theme of the main panel is the zodiac; the twelve astrological signs are clearly depicted, each titled in Hebrew. In the center is

Opposite: Hammath Tiberias synagogue mosaic floor

the sun-god Helios riding his chariot through the heavens. In the four outer corners are busts of female figures symbolizing the seasons. Greek and Aramaic inscriptions list—and bless—the synagogue's leading benefactors; only the word *shalom* appears in Hebrew. Another handsome mosaic pavement, oriented southward, toward Jerusalem, shows the Holy Ark flanked by two lighted seven-branched candelabra, as well as ritual palm branches, incense shovels, and rams' horns, or *shofarim*.

In these mosaics there is an unlikely combination of pagan and Jewish symbols. It is the belief of Professor Moshe Dothan, director of the excavation of the site, that since the synagogue was built at a time when Jewish life was flourishing in Tiberias and the city was the seat of the Sanhedrin (the Jewish high council, or supreme court), its congregants felt secure enough to use the zodiac calendar as a decorative motif. According to Dothan, the Hammath Tiberias synagogue was destroyed in the 5th century, probably by an earthquake. Remains of an earlier synagogue (c. AD 100) and of later ones, from the Byzantine and Early Arab periods, were also found at this site.

The mosaics of the Hammath Tiberias synagogue, among the most beautiful ever found in Israel, are a special attraction. Together with the museum, the ancient bathhouses, and the other archaeological remains, they make this a site of particular interest. A brochure in English describing the excavations is available on request at the entrance to the museum.

Zodiac. Hammath Tiberias synagogue mosaic floor

MUSEUM OF HEROISM

**The Citadel
10 Haganah Street
Acre**

HOURS: Sun.–Thurs. 9:30–17, Fri. 9:30–12, Sat. 9:30–17   TEL.: 04–913900
ADMISSION: $2.50

Focus: **Life and Death in a British Prison**

Here, in the Citadel of Acre—where many of its members had been imprisoned during the last years of the British Mandate—the Underground Prisoners' Association established the Museum of Heroism in 1963. The association also maintains Hechal Hagvurah Museum in Jerusalem (see page 22). The Acre museum's exhibits chronicle the activities of the various Jewish underground organizations in their struggle against British rule in Palestine from 1920 to the time of the establishment of the State of Israel, in 1948.

Located in the northern section of the Old City, the Acre Citadel, built over 12th- and 13th-century Crusader remains, dates from the time of Pasha Ahmad el-Jazzar, the notorious Ottoman governor who controlled most of Palestine and Lebanon from 1775 to his death in 1804. El-Jazzar ("the Butcher") used the Citadel's main tower as his personal residence, and since it was rumored that he kept his vast fortune there, the tower was popularly known in Arabic as Burj el-Khazaneh (Tower of the Treasure). The main hall of the Museum of Heroism is located in this tower, which is entered by way of a narrow bridge across the moat. From the top of this 120-foot tower, the tallest building in Acre, there is a spectacular view of the city and the Mediterranean coastline.

After passing through a handsome Turkish gateway and descending a flight of stairs, visitors reach a large inner courtyard surrounded by cells. During Ottoman times this area was used both as a *kishleh*, or barracks, and as a local jail; in 1875 the Persian religious leader Baha Allah, founder of Bahai, was imprisoned here. During the Mandate period it served as Palestine's highest-security prison.

Photographs, newspaper clippings, and other documents tell the story of

Inner courtyard, Museum of Heroism

the political prisoners held here—and their unceasing struggle against the British authorities. Retold in an exhibit featured in one of the original cells is the daring escape engineered on May 4, 1947, by some of the prisoners with the outside aid of their comrades of the Irgun Tzvai Leumi (National Military Organization), who smuggled explosives into the well-guarded prison. In the end, of the 49 prisoners involved, 29 got away, 9 were killed, and 11 (of whom 3 were later executed in this prison) were recaptured.

Across the courtyard is the gallows. The red uniforms of prisoners condemned to death are displayed in the cell where they spent their last days. Photographs and marble tablets memorialize the 14 members of the Jewish underground executed within these walls by the British authorities. On the floor above are additional cells; in one, the Zionist Revisionist leader Ze'ev (Vladimir) Jabotinsky was held in 1920.

Although the Acre Citadel is in somewhat neglected condition, those interested in the history of Acre and in the activities of the Jewish underground movements will find a visit here a rewarding experience. (Visitors should be prepared for extensive walking.)

NAHARIYA MUNICIPAL MUSEUM

19 Gaaton Street
Nahariya

HOURS: Sun.–Fri. 10–12, Sun. and Wed. 16–18 also

TEL.: 04–922121
ADMISSION: Free

Focus: **History of Nahariya; Regional Archaeology**

The exhibits in this museum, located on the upper floors of Nahariya's municipal building, take two directions: toward the city's modern history and toward regional archaeology. Nahariya was founded in 1935 by Jewish refugees from Germany; its early two-story wooden houses and carefully tended lawns were rare sights in a country where both lumber and water were in short supply. Soon after its establishment, Nahariya was transformed from a small *moshava*, or agricultural settlement, into a popular vacation resort. Its beautiful beaches and well-run pensions and restaurants became famous throughout Palestine. It is still a major vacation spot in Israel.

Photographs and newspaper clippings chronicle the first years of Nahariya and reveal the backgrounds of some of its early settlers. Among the more poignant photographs are those of groups of Jewish veterans of the German army who fought in the Franco-Prussian War of 1870 and in World War I. The founder of the museum, Yisrael Shimoni, had himself served in the German army in World War I. Additional exhibits detail the establishment and development of Nahariya over half a century.

The archaeological section serves as a regional museum for western Galilee. This area, with its rich soil and abundant rainfall, attracted settlers as early as the Paleolithic period—as the hand axes and other prehistoric tools exhibited here testify. The later development of local Canaanite culture can be followed in the displays of Bronze Age pottery and other artifacts excavated in the vicinity. Especially noteworthy are finds from a Middle Bronze Age temple discovered near the seashore. They include a seven-spouted clay cultic vessel, incense burners, and a clay mold for casting the image of a female deity identified as the goddess Astarte, perhaps the patroness of the temple.

One of the most important underwater discoveries of recent times, the sunken remains of a Phoenician vessel, was made off the coast just south of Nahariya. Its cargo included over 250 terra-cotta figurines—some of Tanit, the goddess of Carthage—and many barnacle-encrusted amphorae; these are now on display in the museum.

From later periods come several Roman milestones excavated in Nahariya (one bears the name of Emperor Nero), as well as clay oil lamps, glass vessels, coins, and jewelry found in Roman tombs nearby. On view also are architectural elements from an important Byzantine church excavated on the outskirts of Nahariya.

In addition to archaeological finds, the museum has an extensive collection of seashells. It also houses archives relating to local history and to the history of Central European Jewry.

SASA MUSEUM
Kibbutz Sasa

HOURS: By appointment

TEL.: 06–789067 or 06–988527
ADMISSION: Free

Focus: **Local Archaeology**

High on a hill overlooking the border between Israel and Lebanon is an old stone house that serves as the archaeology museum of Kibbutz Sasa. The collections consist of artifacts discovered in the vicinity. Stone axes from the Paleolithic period provide evidence of early human settlement in the area; clay vessels represent the Bronze and Iron ages; and in an inner courtyard are building stones and column fragments from the Roman and Byzantine periods.

It is important to call ahead, since this small museum can be visited only by appointment.

SHAMIR REGIONAL MUSEUM
Kibbutz Shamir

HOURS: By appointment
TEL.: 06–941941 or 06–947800
ADMISSION: Free

Focus: **Regional Archaeology**

Kibbutz Shamir, on the edge of the Hula Valley, is located in an area rich in archaeological remains. Its museum was established in 1977 by kibbutz member Moshe Kagan to house artifacts found at the many sites of ancient human habitation in the immediate vicinity. Since water is plentiful and the soil is fertile in this part of Upper Galilee, the area has attracted settlers since prehistoric times.

Inside the museum, displays are arranged chronologically, from the Stone Age to the Byzantine period. Maps and photographs accompany the exhibits. Displays include reconstructions of dolmens, the megalithic tomb structures found in abundance around the kibbutz, as well as ancient pillars and capitals from the excavations at nearby Tel Anafa, an important site of the Hellenistic period. From the Roman period are several stone boundary markers that separated the land of one village from another. These markers bear the names of the various ancient localities.

Tools, weapons, and items of daily life from nearly every period are also on display. They include early stone hand axes, flint arrowheads, bronze knives, basalt vessels and grinding stones, and pottery vessels—both local and imported. In addition, the museum's collection features seals, amulets, small statues, jewelry, and oil lamps. Kagan continues to add artifacts to the collections. "My work as a sheepherder gives me the opportunity to wander around, and I know well all the sites in the area," he says.

TEFEN/THE OPEN MUSEUM

Tefen Industrial Park
Kfar Vradim

HOURS: Sun.–Thurs. 9–17, Fri. 9–12, Sat. 10–17

TEL.: 04–977977
ADMISSION: Free

Focus: **Contemporary Sculptures in an Industrial Park**

Altar of Atonement *by Shoshana Hyman*

"Open" in that it is located in a park, and "open" in that it is not governed by any one orthodox aesthetic, this museum was established to bridge, through contemporary art, the distance between industry and technology on the one hand and nature and ecology on the other. The museum was opened to the public in 1987 with about 50 sculptures by Israeli artists placed effectively throughout the grounds of the Tefen Industrial Park, which adjoins Kfar

Going *by*
Ofra Zimbalista

Vradim. The museum facilities include a building for paintings; the exhibits here change periodically. Plans for the future include extending the sculpture garden up to the border of the village of Kfar Vradim and building a hall in the village for the exhibition of graphics.

From the beginning, Stefi Wertheimer, founder and director of both the Tefen enterprise and the Open Museum, consulted with artists and designers regarding the museum's development. It is his hope that other artists will set up their workshops and studios in the Tefen Industrial Park, following the example of a print workshop already established there.

Homage to
Asher *by*
Avraham Ofek

TEL HAI MUSEUM

Kibbutz Tel Hai

HOURS: Sun.–Thurs. 8–17, Fri. 8–13, Sat. 8–17   TEL.: 06–941800
                                                    ADMISSION: $1.50

Focus: **History of Tel Hai, 1907–1920**

The Tel Hai Museum is a large-scale reconstruction of the early-20th-century Jewish settlement that has become a legend in the history of modern Israel. On view within the walled compound are the agricultural implements used by the pioneers who came here in 1907, including a threshing sledge, an oxcart, plows, and branding irons. Inside the restored rooms of the main building is the simple furniture of the time, with an elaborate samovar of the type brought from Russia by the new immigrants.

As the maps, photographs, and text panels here reveal, this area is known as the "finger" of Galilee, since it juts north into the mountains of Lebanon. Half of the water resources of the country flow through it, and it has enormous strategic value. These factors encouraged Zionist pioneers to establish settlements here at the turn of the century: Rosh Pina, Metulla, and Kfar Giladi, as well as Tel Hai. After World War I, despite the efforts of the organization Hashomer (see Beit Hashomer, page 177), several settlements had to be abandoned because of Arab raids. One of the men called upon to revitalize the defense of this part of Galilee was Joseph Trumpeldor, who is memorialized in this museum.

Born in Russia in 1880, Trumpeldor, the first Jewish commissioned officer in the czarist forces, was decorated for his heroic service in the Russo-Japanese War. Trumpeldor joined the Zionist movement and came to Palestine for the first time in 1912. He was later active in establishing the Jewish Battalions during World War I (see Beit Hagedudim, page 133).

Trumpeldor arrived at Tel Hai on March 1, 1920, to help organize its defense, but in an attack by Arabs from a neighboring village several settlers were killed and he was severely wounded. That night, under cover of darkness, the settlers collected the dead and the wounded, set Tel Hai on fire, and retreated toward Kfar Giladi. They were halfway there when Trumpeldor uttered the words *Tov lamoot be'ad artzenu* ("It is good to die for our country") and breathed his last.

The history of this period comes alive in the reconstructed Tel Hai compound through the exhibits of photographs, arms, documents, and other memorabilia. Text panels point out that Trumpeldor's death was not in vain: in October 1920, Tel Hai was rebuilt, and a few months later an agreement

Courtyard with agricultural implements

was signed to transfer the region to the domain of the British Mandate because of the existence in it of Jewish settlements.

Not far from Tel Hai, on the road to Kfar Giladi, is Trumpeldor's grave, located, with the graves of the other casualties of the attack on Tel Hai, at the spot where he died. A statue of a lion, symbol of Trumpeldor's courage, marks the site.

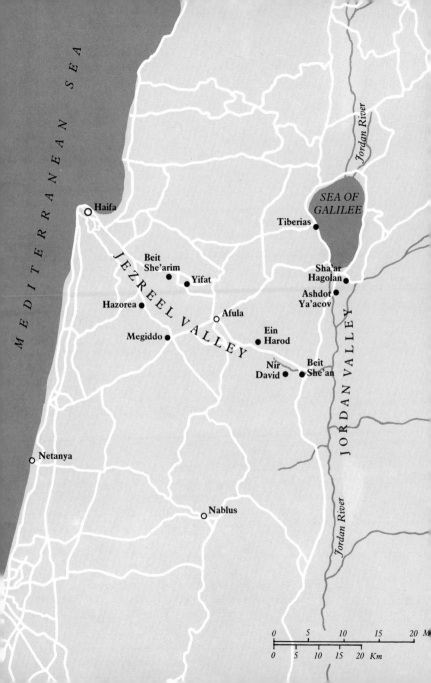

JEZREEL AND JORDAN VALLEYS

BEIT NEHUSHTAN

Kibbutz Ashdot Ya'acov
Jordan Valley

HOURS: Mon., Wed., Fri. 20–21:30, Sat. 10–13 and 20–21:30   TEL.: 06–757737
Also by appointment (call Joseph Keren, 06–757888)   ADMISSION: Free

Focus: **Fine Arts**

Dialogue *by Igael Tumarkin*

This museum was founded in 1958 in memory of two young brothers of Kibbutz Ashdot Ya'acov. Uri lost his life in Israel's War of Independence, in 1948; Rami was felled by the bite of a poisonous snake while working in the kibbutz fields. Since both young men were promising artists, their parents and the other members of the kibbutz decided that the most fitting memorial would be an art museum. Beit Nehushtan serves the population of the Jordan Valley.

The museum's permanent collection includes oils, drawings, textiles, photographs, and sculptures. Exhibitions change every few months, and the museum often hosts special traveling shows loaned by other museums. Both Israeli and international art are featured here, and the permanent collection is growing because every artist exhibited is invited to donate work to the museum. An impressive sculpture by Igael Tumarkin is displayed outside the museum building.

BEIT SHE'AN MUSEUM OF ARCHAEOLOGY

Beit She'an
Jordan Valley

For information call the City Council, 06–586221

Focus: **Local Archaeology**

The Beit She'an Museum is located just north of the city center. If, as seems likely at press time, the museum is still closed for renovation, Beit She'an itself, with its impressive ancient remains, should be visited.

As one of the most important ancient cities in the country, Beit She'an has been continuously occupied for 5,000 years. Located where the Jordan and Jezreel valleys meet, forming the best east–west crossing in the country, it has stood at a major intersection of trade routes since antiquity. After King

Roman amphitheater

Roman baths

Saul died, the Philistines impaled his body on the wall of Beit She'an (1 Samuel 31:10). The main street of the modern city, Rehov Shaul, is dedicated to the king's memory.

During the Hellenistic period the city was renamed Scythopolis in honor of a colony of Scythian mercenaries established here. Under the Romans it became a part of the Decapolis, the powerful league of the ten most important cities in the Eastern Mediterranean. The city's prosperity in this period is evidenced by the well-preserved Roman amphitheater, built about AD 200, which seated 6,000 people. The ongoing archaeological excavations, sponsored by the Ministry of Tourism, the municipality of Beit She'an, the Israel Department of Antiquities and Museums, and the Hebrew University, have also uncovered a city center of the Roman–Byzantine period. Among its features are houses with mosaic floors, a Late Roman nymphaeum, a 2nd-century temple, and a colonnaded street lined with shops.

BEIT SHE'ARIM CATACOMBS AND MUSEUM

**Beit She'arim
Jezreel Valley**

HOURS: Sun.–Thurs. 8–18, Fri. 8–13, Sat. 8–16
Refreshments available at kiosk

TEL.: 04–831643
ADMISSION: $1.50

Focus: **Sarcophagi of the 2nd–4th Century**

The catacombs at Beit She'arim, first explored by Professor Benjamin Mazar in the late 1930s, are among the most important Jewish archaeological monuments in the country. These cave tombs contain many richly decorated stone sarcophagi. A small site museum displaying selected finds from the excavations is housed in an ancient water cistern.

The city of Beit She'arim (House of Gates) flourished during the Late Roman period, when the city served as the seat of the Sanhedrin, the high council, or supreme court, of the Jews. Yehuda Hanasi (Judah the Patriarch), the compiler of the Mishna, lived in Beit She'arim and was buried here, as

Entrance to the catacombs

were his two sons. One of the country's largest synagogues stood in this city; it was demolished by the Romans in the middle of the 4th century.

The catacombs are entered through a partially restored triple-arched façade. Inside, in the labyrinthine corridors and side chambers, are dozens of stone sarcophagi decorated with ornamental motifs such as flowers, trees, birds, animals, and seven-branched candelabra, as well as geometric designs. Inscribed on the sarcophagi are both Hebrew and Greek names of the deceased, some of whom lived in Palestine and some in the Diaspora. Ominous warnings are also seen: an inscription carved on one coffin promises that if any person should ever try to open it, "upon him shall come an evil end"—an ineffective curse, judging from the fact that many of the Beit She'arim sarcophagi were looted centuries ago.

The site museum features thematic displays and exhibits of objects found in the catacombs. Numbers of ancient Hebrew, Aramaic, and Greek inscrip-

Decorated sarcophagus

tions can be perused, and the development of the menorah motif in Jewish art can be traced through nearly 30 distinct variations found here. Other displays highlight the various ornaments and symbols that appear on the sarcophagi—columns, rosettes, ships, a horse and rider—and illustrate traditional Jewish burial customs, from the First Temple period to Talmudic times.

The surrounding park is a pleasant place for a picnic or a light snack.

BEIT STURMAN

Kibbutz Ein Harod
Jezreel Valley

| HOURS: Sun.–Thurs. 8–13, 15–16:30, | TEL.: 06–531605 |
| Fri. 8–12, Sat. 9:30–12:30 | ADMISSION: $2.50 |

Focus: History and Natural History of the Region

This regional museum, founded in 1941, is named after Haim Sturman, a kibbutz member who was killed during the Arab uprising of 1936–39 and whose son and two grandsons fell in subsequent Arab-Israeli conflicts.

Like many other regional museums in Israel, Beit Sturman sees education as its raison d'être and provides wide-ranging programs for schoolchildren. The museum's natural history gallery features collections of local insects, reptiles, mammals—including a two-headed calf—and birds of many species that stop in the Jezreel Valley in their migrations between Europe and their African wintering grounds. Archaeology is also an integral part of the Beit Sturman exhibits; among its many artifacts are 85 Roman milestones—some bearing inscriptions in Greek or Latin—which are set up in the courtyard. Other parts of the museum chronicle the recent history of the area and the development of agriculture and industry in the Jezreel Valley, with special emphasis on the draining of the swamps in the area by kibbutz members after World War I.

The museum's observation deck offers a splendid view of the surrounding Jezreel Valley. The colors of the landscape—dark-green orchards, golden wheat fields, silvery fish ponds—change with the seasons. To the east are the mountains of Gilboa, where the Philistines slew Jonathan and his brothers and King Saul fell upon his sword (I Samuel 31:4).

Kibbutz Ein Harod's art museum, Mishkan Le'omanut, is about 100 yards from Beit Sturman (see page 220).

WILFRID ISRAEL MUSEUM/HOUSE OF ORIENTAL ART

Kibbutz Hazorea
Jezreel Valley

HOURS: Sun.–Fri. 9–12, Sat. 10–12 and 17–18:30   TEL.: 04–899566
ADMISSION: Free

Focus: **Ancient Cultures of the Mediterranean, Egypt, and Iran;**
Regional Archaeology

The collection of Oriental art that is the core of this museum, founded in 1951, was formed by Wilfrid Israel, a German Jew who maintained close relations with Kibbutz Hazorea in its early days and had hoped to settle here and work as a sculptor. He was especially interested in the working possibilities that kibbutzim offered artists. However, during World War II, while on a special mission to aid refugees, Wilfrid Israel was killed when his plane was shot down by the Luftwaffe over the Bay of Biscay. In his will, he left his extensive collection of art from China, India, Cambodia, and Thailand to Kibbutz Hazorea.

On display is a wide array of bronzes, ceramics, and statuettes from various countries of the Far East and also art objects from Egypt, Iran, and the Eastern Mediterranean—arranged so that it is visually easy to follow the development of art during a particular period in places geographically remote from one another. In addition to the permanent collections, the museum features exhibits of arts and crafts, especially by Israeli artists, as well as archaeological finds from the immediate vicinity.

The area around Kibbutz Hazorea is rich in history and archaeological remains, for it lies on the route of the ancient *via maris*, the "Way of the Sea," the overland commercial and military road between Egypt and Mesopotamia. Just 8 miles southeast of the kibbutz is Megiddo, one of the most famous ancient cities along that route, where, according to Revelation 16:16, Armageddon—the final, apocalyptic battle between good and evil—will take place. (Armageddon comes from the Hebrew *Har Megiddo*, "Mountain of Megiddo.")

Megiddo was the site of a decisive battle between Pharaoh Thutmose III and the princes of Canaan in the 15th century BC. It was fortified by King Solomon in the 10th century BC, conquered by Shishak of Egypt about 920 BC, and taken by the Assyrians in 722 BC. Among the impressive remains still visible are fortifications from the Solomonic period, a water system attributed to the kings of the northern kingdom of Israel, granaries, a stable, and a round altar from the mid-3rd millennium BC. A model of the mound, exhibited at the small site museum, helps explain the complicated history of Megiddo.

Head of the Buddha, sandstone, 12th century

MISHKAN LE'OMANUT

Kibbutz Ein Harod
Jezreel Valley

HOURS: Sun.–Thurs. 9–13 and 15–17, Fri. 9–12, Sat. 9–16   TEL.: 06–531670
ADMISSION: $1.50

Focus: Fine Arts; Jewish Folk Art

Mishkan Le'omanut (Temple for the Arts) was established in 1936 by painter Chaim Atar (1902–1953) as the country's first rural art museum. At the beginning just an "art corner" in the small wooden structure that served as Atar's studio, Mishkan Le'omanut was intended to bring art to the people tilling the land, who rarely had an opportunity to visit art museums in the country's major cities.

Entrance to Mishkan Le'omanut

The present galleries, designed by Shmuel Bikeles in 1948, are spacious and especially well illuminated by indirect natural light through the use of hanging double ceilings. They provide a perfect setting for the museum's changing exhibits, which frequently feature outsize paintings, sculptures, and works in mixed media by young Israeli artists.

The museum's permanent collections are wide-ranging. They include Jewish folk crafts and ethnological material from communities throughout the Diaspora, dating from as far back as the 15th century. They also include drawings, paintings, and sculptures by such local artists as Mordechai Ardon, Yossl Bergner, and Shalom of Safed, as well as works by such well-known Jewish artists as Pissarro, Modigliani, and Chagall. Representative paintings of the Impressionist, Realist, Expressionist, and Cubist schools are also on view. The outdoor sculpture garden features works by Jacob Epstein, Chana Orloff, and Igael Tumarkin, among others. The museum's handsome iron gates are the work of Israeli sculptor David Palombo (see Palombo Museum, page 60).

Mishkan Le'omanut maintains an extensive art library, and it sponsors frequent lectures and workshops for adults and youngsters. The quality of the collections and the special light effect in the galleries make this a most interesting place to visit.

Kibbutz Ein Harod's Beit Sturman is about 100 yards away.

MUSEUM OF PIONEER AGRICULTURAL SETTLEMENTS

Kibbutz Yifat
Jezreel Valley

HOURS: Sun.–Thurs. 7–16, Fri. and Sat. 10–13	TEL.: 06–541450
Shaded picnic area nearby	ADMISSION: $1.50

Focus: **Modern Agricultural Settlements in Israel**

Situated on high ground overlooking the Jezreel Valley, this museum utilizes photographs and documentary films to illustrate the way of life of Jewish farmers in Palestine in the late 19th century. The highlight is a full-scale recreation of an early Jewish settlement, including living quarters, workshops, children's nursery, dining room, and communal kitchen. Displays of agricultural implements are arranged chronologically, with demonstrations of harvesting and threshing methods and modes of transportation. From these displays can be deduced the cultural clash brought about by the meeting of traditional Arab farming methods and tools and the more modern implements and agricultural techniques brought to the country by the pioneers from Eastern Europe.

A visit here can be especially enjoyable for families with young children.

MUSEUM OF PREHISTORY AND ETHNOGRAPHY

Kibbutz Sha'ar Hagolan
Jordan Valley

HOURS: Sun.–Thurs. 9–16, Fri. 9–13, Sat. 10–13   TEL.: 06–961350
ADMISSION: $1.25

Focus: **Life at Sha'ar Hagolan, c. 6000 BC**

Interior view

The superb archaeological collection in this small museum features finds from the important prehistoric site of Sha'ar Hagolan, which was discovered accidentally in 1943 when members of Kibbutz Sha'ar Hagolan were digging fish ponds. Surveys and excavations were subsequently conducted by Professor Moshe Stekelis of the Hebrew University, who was the first to recognize the uniqueness of the site. He designated the Neolithic culture that flourished at Sha'ar Hagolan as the Yarmukian culture, after the nearby Yarmuk River, which flows into the Jordan just to the south of the Sea of Galilee.

As the exhibits indicate, this area, which abounds in water, vegetation, and animal life, provided a rich subsistence for prehistoric hunters, fishers, and food-gatherers. The fertile soil also encouraged the development of agriculture and the herding of sheep, cattle, and pigs. While many details of the Yarmukian culture are still uncertain, much can be gleaned from examining the characteristic tools and utensils of flint, limestone, basalt, and clay that were in daily use. Especially intriguing are the many flat river pebbles bearing enigmatic incised symbols.

Head of pottery figurine, 6th millennium BC

There are few other prehistoric sites in the Near East so rich in artistic and religious expression, here represented by elaborate figurines and statuettes. Their high level of craftsmanship sheds dramatic light on the agricultural societies of the 6th millennium BC.

This collection, extensively labeled in both Hebrew and English, was housed in the bomb shelter of the kibbutz until 1982, when it was moved to the present building, designed by architect J. Iwri.

MUSEUM OF REGIONAL AND MEDITERRANEAN ARCHAEOLOGY

Kibbutz Nir David
Jezreel Valley

HOURS: Sun.–Thurs. 8–14, Sat. 10:30–13
Refreshments available at nearby Gan Hashlosha
National Park (Sakhneh)

TEL.: 06–583045
ADMISSION: $2.00

Focus: **Archaeology of the Beit She'an Region, and of Greece, Persia, and Egypt**

The Sakhneh, setting of the Museum of Regional and Mediterranean Archaeology

Close to the route of one of the country's most important ancient roads, over which goods, people, and frequently armies traveled from the Mediterranean basin to the lands of the East, is this fine museum, founded in 1963 by the late Elazar Unger and other members of Kibbutz Nir David, which serves as a regional cultural center.

Warrior Parting from Parents, *black-figured Greek amphora, 4th century* BC

The museum comprises four galleries, one of which is devoted to the art of the classical Greek world. On display here are objects from the collection of Swiss archaeologist and painter Dan Lifschitz, among them geometric, black-figured, and red-figured vases, as well as figurines from Greece and Italy. Another gallery houses Persian art from the 3rd to the 1st millennium BC, with a collection of bowls from Samarkand, and, from Egypt, ancient Coptic textiles.

In another gallery are displayed archaeological finds from the surrounding Beit She'an region. A chronologically arranged selection of artifacts takes the viewer from the Neolithic through the Byzantine period. Among the highlights is a mosaic floor of a synagogue in Beit She'an from the Roman–Byzantine period, with a menorah and a *shofar*. A cross section of a typical tell, or ancient mound (in this case Tel Kitan on the bank of the Jordan River), gives visible form to the archaeological concept of stratigraphy, or superim-

The Abduction of Europa, *clay statuette from Italy, 5th century* BC

posed levels of settlement.

Reconstructed in the museum is a small Bronze Age temple from the same tell. Another interesting exhibit demonstrates ancient weaving techniques, utilizing implements for spinning and weaving discovered in the remains of an Israelite village excavated at the museum site. Vessels from burial caves around Tel Kitan, dating from about 2000 BC, are also on display.

This museum offers admirable educational programs to the local schools and also has a good archaeological library. Exhibits here are clear and well arranged, giving evidence of much thought and professional expertise.

Decorated clay vessels ("chocolate ware") from Tel Kitan

Only a few miles away is the site of the 6th-century AD Beit Alpha synagogue, with a colorful mosaic floor. There is a vivid scene of Abraham preparing to sacrifice Isaac, stopped (visibly) by the hand of God. In the center of the floor is a zodiac wheel, within which the sun-god Helios drives his chariot. The twelve astrological signs are skillfully executed, as are the four seasons, each represented by a female figure. Another scene shows the Ark of the Law flanked by lions, pairs of birds, incense shovels, and a double menorah. It is interesting to compare the iconography of this mosaic floor with that of the mosaic floor of the Hammath Tiberias synagogue (page 198).

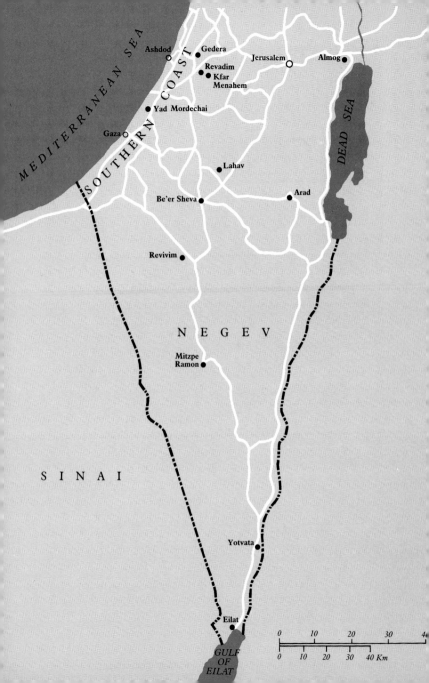

SOUTHERN COAST AND NEGEV

ARAD MUSEUM AND VISITORS CENTER

28 Ben Yair Street
Arad

HOURS: Mon. and Wed. 18–21 (winter 17–19), Sat. 11–13 and 18–20	TEL.: 057–957747 ADMISSION: Free

Focus: **Work of Israeli Artists; Archaeological Discoveries from Tel Arad**

The Arad Museum features exhibits by local artists, each show on view for a month.

Other interests of the museum are the history and archaeology of nearby Tel Arad. This site has been excavated under the directorship of Ruth Amiran on behalf of the Israel Museum, the Israel Exploration Society, and the Department of Antiquities of the State of Israel. Finds at Tel Arad chronicle the development of the ancient city from its establishment, about 3000 BC, in the Early Bronze Age, through the Israelite period, when it served as an important fortress on the road from Edom to Eilat. (The small Israelite temple, with a Holy of Holies, excavated at Tel Arad has been reassembled at the Israel Museum [see page 34].)

In addition to archaeology, the Arad Museum's program includes exhibits on a variety of themes related to the northern Negev and the Judean Desert, among them geography, biology, and ethnography. The history of the planned city of Arad, established in 1963, is also a feature. Audiovisual programs on some of these subjects can be seen at the Visitors Center.

An arts festival takes place in Arad every year, July 5–9. Painters, sculptors, potters, and other artists and craftsmen display their work in the Visitors Center, which remains open from 10 to 22 during the festival.

CORAL WORLD
UNDERWATER OBSERVATORY AND MUSEUM

Eilat

HOURS: Sun.–Thurs. 8:30–16:30, Fri. 8:30–15, Sat. 8:30–16   TEL.: 059–76666
ADMISSION: $6.50

Focus: **Marine Life in the Red Sea**

*Underwater view
from the
observatory*

Situated a few miles south of Eilat, this delightful park offers sights for visitors of all ages. In a series of pools and buildings on the shore of the Red Sea, they can learn about the fish and other forms of marine life unique to this body of water, which extends from the southern tip of Israel all the way south to the Indian Ocean.

Near the entrance are the sea turtle and the stingray pool; farther along is the shark pool, where the sharks can be viewed both from above and from below the water's surface. The highlight of Coral World is its underwater observatory, entered by way of a spiral staircase at the end of a long pier. In this circular observation post built in the midst of a coral reef, visitors can peer through a series of windows and see schools of fish in their natural habitat, swimming in and out through a forest of coral.

The indigenous species of fish, which appear in a seemingly infinite variety of shapes and colors, include yellow long-nosed butterfly fish; triangular Moorish idols with bands of red, black, and white; and puffers with sloping snouts and orange spots. Most impressive of all are the lionfish, with their long and colorful (and very venomous) spines, their dorsal fins creating the illusion of dancers' veils.

Back on shore, the one-room museum is overshadowed by the aquarium, with its rich collection of fish from other parts of the world. The most dramatic part of the aquarium is a dimly lighted room where hundreds of phosphorescent plants, fish, and other denizens of the sea glow in the dark.

HOUSE OF THE SCRIBE

Kibbutz Almog
Jericho Junction

HOURS: Sun.–Fri. 9–16 (Note: call in advance.)	TEL.: 02–228465
	ADMISSION: $2.00

Focus: Replicas of the Dead Sea Scrolls

Kibbutz Almog is situated near the northwestern shore of the Dead Sea, close to Qumran and the caves where the Dead Sea Scrolls were found. The House of the Scribe, devoted to the ancient Essene community of Qumran and the scrolls that its members produced, is a room beneath the dining hall of the kibbutz that once served as a bomb shelter.

Exhibited here are both photographic and handwritten reproductions of the Dead Sea Scrolls, as well as some ancient jars and other clay vessels discovered in the Qumran excavations. Texts, panels, photographs, and architectural drawings of Qumran explain the background of the Essenes and their writings. The House of the Scribe also pays tribute to the person who first recognized the archaeological importance of the scrolls—Professor Eliezer Sukenik, one of the founders of modern Israeli archaeology.

Rivaling in interest the modest exhibit in this small museum are the seeming parallels between the communal life-styles of the ancient sect of the Essenes and the modern kibbutz: their efforts to establish an egalitarian community and to cultivate the surrounding arid desert land. (There were no women, however, at Qumran.) A guided tour of the kibbutz is available for a small fee.

In addition to the site of Qumran, on the western shore of the Dead Sea there are several important points of interest. About 10 miles to the south is the oasis of Ein Gedi, with its impressive archaeological remains from the Chalcolithic period, the Iron Age, and the Byzantine period—as well as clearly marked hiking trails through the spectacular gorges of the Judean Wilderness. Still farther south is Masada, Israel's most famous archaeological monument, an essential stop on any itinerary.

MA'AYAN MUSEUM

Rehov Ha'avot
Be'er Sheva

HOURS: Sun.–Thurs. 9–13

TEL.: 057–79754
ADMISSION: Free

Focus: Making Jewish Ritual Objects

It is the purpose of this small museum to increase the understanding of processes involved in the making of ritual articles connected with Jewish worship and to explain the concepts behind the processes. Exhibits show, for example, the stages in the transformation of the skin of a goat, from the time that the animal is slaughtered, into a surface on which a scribe can write holy texts. The *shofar*—the instrument that was sounded in ancient days to announce the approach of the Sabbath and is sounded today in synagogues on the high holy days—is the subject of another exhibit. The process of molding a ram's horn into a *shofar* by the application of heat is shown, and incidentally it is explained that a cow's horn may not be used because of the connection with the golden calf (Exodus 32). Other items used by observant Jews, such as the *tefillin*, or phylacteries, and the *tallit*, or prayer shawl, are on display, along with illustrations of all the concrete steps involved in turning the raw materials into finished articles.

MAKHTESH RAMON VISITORS CENTER

Mitzpe Ramon National Park

HOURS: Sun.–Thurs. 9–16:30, Fri. 9–14:30, Sat. 9–16:30

TEL.: 057–88691
ADMISSION: $2.50

Focus: Geological Phenomena of a Desert Crater

Makhtesh Ramon is one of the world's largest crater-like depressions: it is 25 miles long, 5½ miles wide, and 1,300 feet deep. Visitors to this center have the opportunity to become familiar with diversified geological phenomena as well as to enjoy the scenic landscape of open desert and scenic canyons. The nature reserve covers an area of 250,000 acres and contains archaeological

Following pages: Makhtesh Ramon Visitors Center overlooking the desert crater

sites from the Canaanite, Judean, Nabataean, Roman, and Byzantine periods. Hiking trails are marked by subject: geology, animal observation, geochemistry, and more. All paths lead to dramatic observation points.

The circular Visitors Center is built out of local stone that blends well with the landscape. It overlooks the gigantic crater, and its exhibits provide an introduction to the natural history of the area. Large backlighted transparencies and photomurals of desert life highlight some of the 1,200 species of plants that grow in the desert, as well as the area's indigenous birds of prey, reptiles, foxes, gazelles, ibex, and wolves. The geology of the crater is explained by pictorial and descriptive text panels; these are complemented by large samples of local basalt, sandstone, mudstone, quartzite, limestone, and chalk.

Scientific research relating to the geology and ecology of the crater is conducted in the laboratories and classrooms of the nearby Ramon Nature Reserve Campus. This educational facility is dedicated to the memory of General Yekutiel Adam, a man who was deeply concerned with conserving Israel's natural resources and protecting the environment.

Interior view, Makhtesh Ramon Visitors Center

MITZPE REVIVIM MUSEUM
Kibbutz Revivim

HOURS: Sun.–Thurs. 9–15, Sat. 10:30–12:30
and 15:30–17:30

TEL.: 057–965249
ADMISSION: $1.50

Focus: History of Kibbutz Revivim

Wireless operator, Mitzpe Revivim Museum, Kibbutz Revivim

Site of the 1948 battleground, with Mitzpe Revivim in the background

The restored fort that served as the living quarters of the founders of Kibbutz Revivim now houses its museum. Around the inner courtyard are the rooms, left more or less as they were some forty years ago.

As the exhibits here set forth, Kibbutz Revivim, isolated amid the inhospitable sands of the Negev, about 40 minutes by car from Be'er Sheva, was established in 1943 by a group of young people of the Labor Youth Movement whose purpose was to conduct agricultural experiments and to assess the possibility of further Jewish settlement in the Negev. With them came an agronomist and an engineer, who was to build an irrigation system for raising crops. The name they chose is a sign of their optimism, given the harsh semiarid environment: *revivim* is the Hebrew word for "showers" or "light rain."

The summer of 1943 was a difficult time: the German siege of Stalingrad, the doomed uprising in the Warsaw ghetto, Rommel fast advancing toward Palestine. Most dismaying, the full dimension of the Holocaust was becoming known. Chronicled in the exhibits here is the saga of how the members of Revivim continued their work—their struggles, their failures and successes, the routine of their daily life.

The scene remains as it was: the dining room, where the tables are set with tin plates, cutlery, and kettles; the kitchen, with its large cooking utensils; the ammunition room; the engineer's hut, with its drawing board; the club room, with a battery-operated radio, a gift from Ben-Gurion. The personnel are represented by mannequins: in the sleeping quarters a soldier snores peacefully on one of the cots, while in an adjoining room a female wireless operator sends and receives messages regarding the Egyptian advance on Revivim during Israel's War of Independence, in 1948.

The museum also features a collection of early farm implements and photographs portraying the daily life of 19th- and 20th-century Jewish settlers in Palestine. From the top of the five-story observation tower (Heb. *mitzpe*) can be seen a panoramic view of the surrounding area. This interesting museum provides an enjoyable way to brush up on history.

MUSEUM FOR BEDUIN CULTURE
Kibbutz Lahav

HOURS: Sat.–Thurs. 9–15, Fri. 9–12

TEL.: 057–961597
ADMISSION: $2.00

Focus: **Daily Life of the Beduin in the Negev and Sinai**

The Museum for Beduin Culture was opened to the public in 1985. Kibbutz Lahav, where it is located, is surrounded by wheatfields; after the harvest, groups of Beduin arrive and dot the area with their black tents while their flocks nibble at the gleanings. The traditional nomadic way of life is, however, fast disappearing as more and more of the Beduin of the Negev settle down in permanent housing. The Museum for Beduin Culture is devoted to preserving and recording the vanishing Beduin crafts and customs. It is what curator Orna Goren calls a "last-minute museum."

The museum's circular, tentlike building houses an extraordinary collection of Beduin folk art, tools of daily life, and textiles. Lifelike exhibits demonstrate such traditional Beduin activities as weaving goat hair into a carpet on a hand loom, baking flat loaves of pita bread, and playing the *rabába*, a stringed instrument. Several unique women's outfits are on display, complete with bead-and-coin-bedecked face veils. Vying with these in splendor are the elaborate trappings of the wedding camel, transporter of the nuptial gifts. A model of a sheikh's tomb sheds light on Beduin burial customs. The favorite of many visitors is a display of toys ingeniously fashioned by the Beduin from discarded cans, wire, and just ordinary junk. Throughout the museum, clear and extensive labels appear in Arabic, English, and Hebrew.

Near the exit is a showcase with clothes worn by the Jabiliyya tribe in the

Beduin woman weaving

mountains of Sinai. Embroidered dresses in the traditional style are displayed alongside newer ones garishly decorated with plastic beads. The contrast points up the changes in Beduin material culture that have occurred in the last few decades.

An exhibit of local archaeological finds is on view at the Joe Alon Center, close by. Most of the material is from Tel Halif, the probable site of biblical Ziklag (Joshua 15:31; I Samuel 25:6).

With a little luck, visitors may be invited to partake of fresh-brewed coffee in the Beduin tent adjacent to the museum. There, sitting on pillows, they can sip their coffee while enjoying traditional Beduin music and stories.

If notified in advance, Kibbutz Lahav can provide lunch for individuals or groups in its dining room.

Brewing coffee in Beduin tent

MUSEUM FOR THE HISTORY OF GEDERA AND THE BILUIM

1 Pines Street
Gedera

HOURS: Sun.–Fri. 8:30–14 (Tues. and Thurs. 16–18 also)   TEL.: 08–593316
ADMISSION: $1.00

Focus: Settlement of Gedera

This museum, housed in a turn-of-the-century building, records the history of Gedera through photographs, documents, and text panels. That history began in Russia in the wake of the bloody pogroms of 1881, after which a group of Jewish students, thirteen boys and one girl, left the city of Kharkov for Palestine. Despairing of ever gaining equality in Russia, they declared in their manifesto: "We want a home in our country. It was given to us by the mercy of God and registered in the archives of history." The group took the name Bilu, from the initials of the words *beit Ya'acov lechu venelcha* ("House of Jacob, come ye, let us go"; Isaiah 2:5). These high school and university students were the first Zionist settlers who came to till the Promised Land. Others followed, mostly young middle-class Russian intellectuals like themselves. This initial wave of immigration to Palestine (1882–1903) became known as the First Aliyah.

The first Bilu pioneers, or Biluim, encountered many unexpected delays as they tried to learn the techniques of farming at the agricultural school at Mikveh Israel and met with a near disaster in a premature attempt to settle at Rishon Lezion (see Rishon Lezion History Museum, page 120). Yet on the second day of Hanukkah in 1884, members of the original group established the settlement of Gedera, clearing a cave for their living quarters; they were equipped with only a gun, a dog, and eight picks. They had little food, the waters were brackish, the neighbors hostile. They became ill and left for Jaffa. Yet eventually they returned.

Exhibited photographs show the first hut, built by Yehiel Michael Pines, as well as the community's later structures, including a flour mill, a wine cellar, the first school, and the first synagogue. Other displays feature the contribution of subsequent settlers at Gedera: a group of Yemenite immigrants who came in 1912, a group from Poland who arrived in 1928, and the 50 families from Germany who established their own neighborhood in Gedera between 1933 and 1939. The current population of Gedera stands at approximately 7,000.

Museum for the History of Gedera and the Biluim

This museum is a modest monument to the early settlers' tenacity and hard work.

MUSEUM OF THE NEGEV

1 Ha'atzmaut Street
Be'er Sheva

HOURS: Sun., Tues., Wed. 8:30–14, Mon. and Thurs. 8:30–16   TEL.: 057–34338
ADMISSION: $1.00

Focus: 4,000 Years of Archaeology in the Negev

The Museum of the Negev is located in the oldest part of Be'er Sheva, a city mentioned frequently in the Bible as the home of the patriarchs; it was the place where Abraham settled his dispute over a well (Heb. *be'er*) with Abimelech, ruler of the Negev, by giving him seven (Heb. *sheva*) ewes (Genesis 21:25–33).

This museum, which was founded in 1953, is easily identified by its slim minaret, since it is housed in a former Ottoman mosque built around the turn of the century. The main archaeological exhibitions are located in the mosque's open courtyard and domed central hall. Finds ranging in date from the 4th millennium BC to the 8th century AD come from excavations at such nearby sites as Tel Be'er Sheva and Tel Arad, which are open to the public.

Among the earliest objects exhibited are flint tools, clay and copper vessels, and tiny ivory figures from the Chalcolithic period. Also displayed are weapons, clay storage jars and other vessels, and statuettes—as well as a reconstructed four-horned altar—from the Israelite levels of Tel Be'er Sheva, which was an important fortress and administrative center for the kings of Judah between the 10th and the 6th century BC. In addition to site plans and photographs, the museum has a scale model of a royal storehouse from the time of King Hezekiah, about 700 BC.

The Hellenistic, Roman, and Byzantine periods of the Negev are well represented by glass and ceramic vessels, oil lamps, jewelry, coins, and architectural elements. Especially interesting are some elaborate mosaics of the Byzantine period. One of the most important, from a church at nearby Kissufim, bears a Greek inscription with a precise date of dedication—the kind of chronological clue that is the dream of every archaeologist. Translated, the date is August 4 in the year 576.

The museum also features temporary exhibits of finds from area excavations, which are better presented than the permanent collections. Most labels are in Hebrew. In general, maintenance and housekeeping are minimal. The museum has a reading room and a small research library, available to students and interested visitors.

A climb up the spiral staircase inside the minaret leads to an unobstructed view of Be'er Sheva and its environs.

REVADIM ARCHAEOLOGICAL MUSEUM
Kibbutz Revadim

HOURS: By appointment

TEL.: 08–591063
ADMISSION: Free

Focus: **Archaeological Finds from Tel Miqne**

At the entrance to Kibbutz Revadim stands a hall, completed in 1988, where finds from the ongoing excavations at nearby Tel Miqne are displayed. The site has been tentatively identified with biblical Ekron, one of the five major Philistine cities. The Canaanites occupied Tel Miqne until the appearance of the Sea Peoples, about 1200 BC; two centuries later King David won a major victory against the Philistines here, after he smote Goliath: "And the men of Israel and Judah arose, and shouted, and pursued the Philistines, until thou comest to Gai, and to the gates of Ekron. And the wounded of the Philistines fell down by the way of Shaarim, even unto Gath, and unto Ekron" (I Samuel, 17:52). The city was besieged by the Assyrians in 712 BC and totally destroyed by the Babylonians a century later.

Maps, models, excavation plans, and quotations from the Bible and other sources recount the history of the city. A large chart traces the Assyrian campaigns against the Philistines, whose cities stood on the coastal route to Egypt. Decorated clay vessels and shards, found at Tel Miqne and at other Philistine sites, show ornamental motifs of Aegean origin.

The production of olive oil and weaving were major industries in the region during the Israelite period, especially in the 7th century. Over 100 oil presses were discovered at Tel Miqne, as well as hundreds of loom weights. Finds from that period on display at the museum include a reconstructed oil press, clay jars for exporting oil, iron agricultural tools, and four-horned stone altars.

SHEPHELA REGIONAL MUSEUM
Kfar Menahem

HOURS: Sun.–Fri. 9–12:30, Sat. 13–14

TEL.: 08–591577
ADMISSION: $3.50

Focus: **Regional Archaeology of the Shephela**

A teaching institution, the Shephela Regional Museum, founded in 1941, was the first wholly youth-oriented museum in Israel. A small collection of Stone Age flint implements found around Kfar Menahem by kibbutz members while sowing clover in the surrounding fields fascinated the youngsters of the kibbutz, and the idea of a youth museum was born. More than 200 school-children participate in the museum's planned activities every day.

Several buildings scattered throughout the kibbutz make up the museum. They include a pavilion for paintings and sculpture, a gallery for special loan exhibits from the Israel Museum, and a permanent archaeology section featuring well-arranged collections of antiquities found in the region. Individual labels here are only in Hebrew, but the long explanatory text panels are in both Hebrew and English.

The most impressive aspect of the museum is the participatory exhibits jointly planned and executed by youngsters and curators. A wide variety of resources is presented here: books, a playhouse, a puppet theater, costumes, a ceramic workshop. Young visitors may, for example, encounter a forest populated by well-known characters from children's literature.

In a ceramic workshop, children can wander around exhibits and touch many of the displayed objects. Here, too, direct participation is encouraged and the young visitors can try their hands at forming their own creations from clay.

This museum's creative displays and programming are designed by kibbutz member Moshe Israel; he and the other curators believe that active participation is the way to "avoid stereotypes and achieve individuality in children's work." The museum also provides written study materials on every subject covered, and it conducts seminars for local teachers throughout the year.

The Shephela Regional Museum has special attractions for both children and adults.

YAD MORDECHAI MUSEUM

Kibbutz Yad Mordechai

HOURS: Daily 8–17

TEL.: 051–20528
ADMISSION: $1.50

In this place
Seek and look for what can be seen no more,
Hear voices that can be heard no more
Understand—
What is beyond all understanding.
—Inscription on a wall of the museum

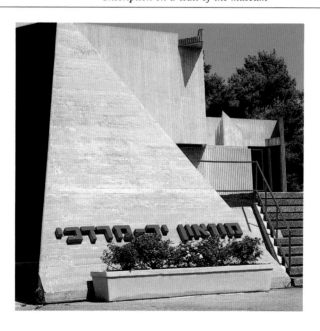

Housed in a somber concrete building, the chronologically arranged exhibits in Yad Mordechai Museum begin in the area below ground level with an overview of more than 1,000 years of Jewish life in Central and Eastern Europe. Largely it is the story of the *shtetl*—of the small towns of Eastern Europe, where Jewish tailors, bakers, tinsmiths, farmers, peddlers, grocers, merchants, and moneylenders, all students of the Torah, created a way of life and left their stamp on Jewish thinking and learning, faith and education.

In the dimly lighted exhibition area on the ground floor, displays document the rise of the Nazis—the boycotting of Jewish shops, the book burnings, the desecration of synagogues and shattering of shop windows on Kristallnacht, and the ominous legislation requiring all Jews to wear yellow stars. Another exhibit relates to the outbreak of World War II, on September 1, 1939, when Hitler's forces invaded Poland. "They were not Huns," reads a text panel, "nor ignorant Cossacks. They came from the land of poets and philosophers, in the middle of the 20th century." The testimony of an eyewitness is presented: "In Auschwitz I saw a mother from whose arms three small children were wrenched and thrown into the wagon. Her scream was so terrifying that even the German officer was struck. He told her she could save one—only one. But she just stood there frozen, unable to choose one and let the others die. They were all taken to death."

In another section of the museum the events of the 1943 Warsaw ghetto uprising unfold: the first clash with the Germans, on January 18, 1943, when a group of Jews about to be transported opened fire on their guards and escaped; the entrance of the Nazis into the ghetto to put down the uprising, on April 19, 1943; the five weeks of fighting, until the last Jewish defenders were dead. Among them was Mordechai Anilewitz, in whose memory Kibbutz Yad Mordechai is named. He was killed in his bunker at 18 Mila Street on May 8, 1943. In his last letter, shown here with his photograph, he wrote: "My life's aspiration is fulfilled. The Jewish self-defense has arisen. Blissful and chosen is my fate, to be among Jewish fighters in the ghetto."

Other resistance fighters and partisan leaders are honored through photographs and a memorial wall with the names of Jewish fighting groups. Documentary material includes some rare copies of the *Partisan Press*, printed by and for the resistance fighters in the forests of Rodniki. The museum's collections also cover the story of the immigration of many resistance fighters to Palestine after the close of World War II. One exhibit here deals with the clandestine immigration (see Clandestine Immigration and Naval Museum, page 150). Another exhibit chronicles the establishment of eleven Jewish settlements in the southern coastal plain—including Kibbutz Yad Mordechai—on the night of Yom Kippur in 1946.

On the top floor of the museum there is a detailed reconstruction of the crucial battle that took place in May 1948, when Kibbutz Yad Mordechai was cut off from the rest of Israel by the Egyptian invasion and later recaptured.

The structure and interior layout of the museum, designed in 1968 by father and son architects Arieh and Eldad Sharon, have an integral share in recreating the historic events remembered here.

YOTVATA MUSEUM AND VISITORS CENTER

Kibbutz Yotvata

HOURS: Sun.–Thurs. 9–14:30, Fri. 9–13, Sat. 10–14

TEL.: 059–76018

ADMISSION: $1.50

Refreshments (including dates, yogurt, and ice cream produced at the kibbutz) available at the café

The human and natural history of the Arava—the arid section of the Great Rift Valley that extends southward from the Dead Sea to the Red Sea—is the focus of this beautiful, well-designed museum, located across the road from Kibbutz Yotvata. The kibbutz itself is situated near perennial springs that create an oasis in otherwise desolate surroundings. The Arava's wide variety

Dedicatory inscription for the Citadel at Yotvata, 293–305

of indigenous plants and animal life is presented through actual-size dioramas of the region's various environments.

The lower level of the museum features archaeological exhibits, including finds from Kuntillet Ajrud, an Iron Age cultic center in the Sinai. Here, also, the techniques of ancient copper smelting at the nearby Timna copper

Demonstration of ancient smelting techniques

mines can be studied: black-and-white drawings and models of the furnace and primitive blow bellows illustrate the process of casting molten copper in vessel molds hewed out of stone. A well-selected series of engraved landscapes of the area is accompanied by appropriate biblical quotations, and a 15-minute slide show on the Timna Valley, available in Hebrew, English, and German, provides a pleasant summation of this exceptionally attractive exhibit.

A visit to Yotvata should be followed by a stop at the ancient site of Timna, some 15 miles north of Eilat, where remains of Egyptian copper mines and smelting installations of the 13th–11th century BC and a fortified camp were discovered. Two shrines to the Egyptian goddess Hathor, divine patroness of mines, were excavated nearby. An Egyptian hieroglyphic inscription and a relief of Ramses III offering a sacrifice to the goddess can be seen on the face of a beautiful wind-carved cliff near King Solomon's Pillars, the most famous of the vividly colored natural sandstone formations in the area.

MUSEUMS BY SUBJECT

ART

Jerusalem
The Israel Museum 25
L.A. Mayer Memorial Institute for
    Islamic Art 48
Museum for Islamic Art 51
Museum of Jewish Art 53
Palombo Museum 60
Ticho House 67
Yad Vashem 75

Tel Aviv
Rubin Museum 99
Helena Rubinstein Pavilion 102
Tel Aviv Museum of Art 103

Tel Aviv Environs
Ben Ari Museum, Bat Yam 116
Mishkan Le'omanut, Holon 118
Museum of Israeli Art, Ramat
    Gan 118
Ryback Museum, Bat Yam 123
Yad Lebanim Museum, Herzliya 126
Yad Lebanim Museum, Petah

Tikva 127

Sharon Coastal Region
Janco–Dada Museum, Ein Hod 142

Haifa
Haifa Museum 155
Mané-Katz Museum 162
Museum of Japanese Art/Tikotin
    Museum 163

Galilee
Bar David Institute of Jewish Art,
    Kibbutz Bar'am 173
Tefen/The Open Museum, Kfar
    Vradim 206

Jezreel and Jordan Valleys
Beit Nehushtan, Kibbutz Ashdot
    Ya'acov 212
Wilfrid Israel Museum, Kibbutz
    Hazorea 218
Mishkan Le'omanut, Kibbutz Ein
    Harod 220

ARCHAEOLOGY

Jerusalem
The Burnt House 14
The Citadel Museum of the History
    of Jerusalem 16
Franciscan Biblical Museum 19
Greek Orthodox Patriarchate
    Museum 21
The Israel Museum 25
Museum for Islamic Art 51
Rockefeller Museum 61
Siebenberg House 64
The Skirball Museum 65

Wohl Archaeological Museum 70
Bible Lands Museum
    Jerusalem 79

Tel Aviv
Antiquities Museum of Tel Aviv–
    Yafo 83
Eretz Israel Museum 90

Tel Aviv Environs
Beit Miriam Museum, Kibbutz
    Palmahim 115

ETHNOGRAPHY AND FOLK ART

HISTORY

SCIENCE, TECHNOLOGY, AND NATURE

MUSEUMS LISTED ALPHABETICALLY